LIVING
IN THE
LIGHT

640 4061

4669030

ABCXBCA 20
Wausmy 20
X

5857
934
1880

WWWLWW

God is Still
working your Story.
Quit Trying to
Steal the pen

Trust the Author!

Keldrick

Jeff Robins

LIVING IN THE LIGHT

BECOMING CONFIDENT IN YOUR PURPOSE
BY SEEING YOURSELF, OTHERS,
AND GOD MORE CLEARLY

Cathy L. Tonking

LIFEWISE BOOKS

LIVING IN THE LIGHT
Becoming Confident in Your Purpose by Seeing Yourself,
Others, and God More Clearly
By Cathy L. Tonking

Published by:

LIFEWISE BOOKS

PO BOX 1072
Pinehurst, TX 77362
LifeWiseBooks.com

To contact the author: cathytonking.com

ISBN (Print): 978-1-952247-62-0
ISBN (Ebook): 978-1-952247-63-7

DEDICATION

To all of my children, both natural and spiritual, and the generations to come who desire to know God, themselves and others better.

CONTENTS

INTRODUCTION

It wasn't until I was an adult that I came to value my contribution to the world. It would take a journey of discovery to unravel what my gift to the world looked like. I was always a faithful person; I believed in God. However, my God had many different identities as I grew into adulthood. Finding the God of my family legacy for myself is what positively changed my view of God, others, and myself. It is my desire to share my journey of faith with you, as my contribution in a world of spiritual uncertainty by keeping the legacy of faith alive. It has been on my heart for a few years to write a book of faith, hope, and love for the next generation. This is the story of my journey into matters of the heart. All spiritual realities are matters of the heart, not the head. No wonder we are admonished to pay careful attention to what goes in our hearts: "Above all else, guard your heart, for everything you do flows from it."[1]

As I sit writing this book, we have been in the middle of a worldwide pandemic where there has been much pain and suffering. This has caused many to fear, experience confusion, and become isolated. Have you ever been through a rough time? Maybe it felt like the situation around you would never change. A pandemic can unleash bizarre nightmares and increased confusion that changes the soul's landscape. We can find ourselves in places and circumstances where we feel helpless and without hope. Many of us have felt stuck in our homes, stuck in our lives, in need of help or direction.

Maybe you are struggling in a darkness of sorts and wonder if light will find you. Maybe you have even cried out to God for deliverance from your current situation. It seems like no better time than when people are feeling hopeless about the future to release what has taken me a lifetime to understand about learning how to live in the light. I have led a faithful life for over thirty years, and I have come to understand the power of grace and God's love for each one of us. My intent in writing this book is that God's light will shine in you and show you what he wants to do in and through your life.

We live in a culture that doesn't understand that to God darkness and light are alike. We like the light and don't like the darkness, but the God who is with us in the darkest of days *is* the true light. The darkness doesn't disturb him at all. He created it. God shines brightest in the dark and brings truth and healing into our lives when the secrets of our hearts are brought into the light.

If you are willing to go on a journey with me, you will see that God is faithful to protect you and lead you into greater and greater light. You can live with the light turned on even in the midst of darkness. During the hard times, we tend to look deeper into life's meaning and find that we really do need God. Sometimes it takes a crisis or a worldwide phenomenon to give us a reset. We can, by intention, create a purposeful life when we are willing to look again, as a young adult, at a life with God.

I have divided this book into three sections: Life with Myself, Life with Others, and Life with God to allow you moments in time to consider where you are, where you're going, and who it is that is going with you. The truth is, coming into adulthood can be a time of great uncertainty, especially when it comes to living life with ourselves, life with others, and life with God. Let's dig into some truths.

LIFE WITH ME

This is where we will discuss our gifts, talents, personalities, and uniquenesses. For many of us, the second decade of life is a time of self-discovery. When I was a young adult, it was only natural that my focus was more on myself. Self-focus can sound like a bad thing, especially in a culture that promotes the importance of image, career, and how many likes we get on social media. That is not the kind of self-focus I am talking about. Sometimes self-focus can be good. When we look to grow into the life that God has for us, we are able to consider and love our lives, just as we are.

LIFE WITH OTHERS

It seems that we start out our lives living with those we are most comfortable with. As we grow and mature, we become aware of other relationships around us that are not so comfortable. I remember as I grew in my relationships with others outside of my immediate family, significant challenges came with them; some of which I was not prepared to handle. There were also relationships where I was hurt and offended. It is in the pain and suffering of our own brokenness and the brokenness of others that we become aware of our need for grace. And with the discovery of grace comes the realization of our need for God.

Life with others will always require forgiveness, which many, many times is just too hard. We don't need to wait for those who have hurt us, wounded us, and betrayed us to apologize. Why? Because forgiveness heals *us*. Learning what forgiveness is and what it isn't will enable us to live lives of greater freedom and destiny. We will learn how to let go of the baggage we carry from the past and step into the life that God has for us.

LIFE WITH GOD

Life can leave us stumbling in the dark at times, when we aren't aware that there is a way out. It took me many years of disappointments, ups, and downs to come to a place where I could take an honest look at myself and what I believed. I had to learn to become comfortable in my own skin and that meant I needed to see myself through a higher lens. I needed to be exactly where I was and stop trying to be something I was not. I had to develop a greater knowledge of myself, others, and God so I could walk into a full life. I needed the light turned on. I needed a spiritual awakening.

What is a spiritual awakening? I believe it means to wake up to God and to come out from the darkness into God's glorious light. There comes a time in all of our lives when we realize we are not as spiritually awake as we thought we were. It is a time when we realize that everything we think we know about God, may actually be our own opinions. It's a time when we need wisdom that comes from his Word. We need spiritual mothers and fathers to help put a frame around God and provide a filter for us to see him for who he really is. Spiritual mentors are those who have come to know, recognize, be conscious of, and understand God who has existed from the beginning. No matter your age, God will keep you from stumbling and be with you, but you must recognize the lighted path and the one who is waking you up.

Who is this God? "God is the one who carries you from your birth, supported you from the moment you left the womb and keeps carrying you! He says I am your Maker and your Caregiver. I will carry you and be your Savior."[2] God wants to save you from living just for yourself.

He wants to show you how to live with others and with himself. Why do we need to live with God? "Lovers of God walk on the highway of light, and their way shines brighter and brighter until they bring forth the perfect day. But the wicked walk-in thick darkness, like those who travel in fog, and yet don't have a clue why they keep stumbling."[3] God has come to shine his light upon you. So that even in the dark you are not alone, and you can find your way.

YOUR JOURNEY

Your journey into a spiritual awakening is not simply a one-time occurrence. You will experience God when he wakes you up and shines his light upon you. Your life with God becomes a process of growing from light to greater light, and the person you are today is not who you will be in the next decade of your life. You will grow and go through times and seasons of gradual awakenings. You will experience different cycles and expressions where you move from darkness to light.

Life is made up of darkness and light, and to God they are the same. God not only comes to shine his light upon you when you wake up in this one-time occurrence but you will need to go from one brighter level of God's glory to take you to another. You will need the light turned on and for it to stay on. This is called living a transformational life that will take God and others together to walk with you and remind you to keep the light turned on.

LIVING A LIFE OF PURPOSE

God has a purpose for you and that is to make you like him. He wants to pour into you the brightness of his light, by giving you a lantern and a compass, so you can find your way to him and to your destiny. God wants to place you in a space where you can operate in your full stride. There are countless ways of getting there and many different plans, but one purpose, and that is to fill the earth with the splendor of God, so that the world can truly be a beautiful place. Living in the decade between twenty and thirty years of age is an exciting and scary time. There are so many changes that take place in this third decade. You will leave school, find a job, embark on a career…and you may find someone to commit your life to. There are so many changes that can leave you looking for a vision or a destination where you are able to place your feet firmly on solid ground.

Years ago, I was looking for inspiration and motivation to discover my purpose. What I really needed was to see myself as God saw me and to see what others saw in me. I needed to get a clear view of myself. This would teach me how to do life with myself, life with others, and how to have a life with God.

Greater vision opens opportunities for finding our God-given assignments where we can serve the world around us with our gifts, talents, personalities, and God-given destinies. When I use the word *destiny*, I am referring to the God-given design that we are created for. The place where we can admit that we haven't acquired all that we are pursuing but can run with passion into the abundance that comes when God makes us his own. It is a journey, a process of discovery, where we reach to God who is reaching out to us. And in this partnership, the world becomes a better place and our lives are enriched.

This is not meant to be a self-help book to discover your purpose; rather, it is an invitation to go on a journey with God and others to discover a life that is fulfilling and alive. You may not know what your assignment is right now, but that is not the point. God has given each of us an assignment. When you see yourself, others, and God more clearly, this will help you in the process of becoming your authentic self.

That assignment will ebb and flow and develop. You may have been told to figure out your life or to get your life together, but that is impossible alone. You don't have to go it alone. You were never meant to be alone in the dark, or isolated. The truth is that there is a light that God wants to shine on you so that you can see yourself and the world more clearly. Life with Myself, Life with Others, and Life with God are the three keys that have helped me navigate through this gift called life. We have one life to live, and we are all becoming something. You are special to God, and you can become something special and unique to the world around you. God created you with beauty and purpose. God has a place where you can find your significance, grow in confidence, and have access to his power to transform you into his masterpiece.

LIVING A LEGACY

You and I were born to leave a legacy. A legacy is not only what you leave behind but also what you inherit. There are values, beliefs, skills, and attitudes that get passed down to each generation, and there are things still left to be inherited. I am not a philosopher. I am not a theologian. I am a faith-filled spiritual mother who believes that God loves legacy. Proverbs 13:22 says, "A good man (and woman) leaves an inheritance to his (her) children's children."[4] I believe that what we paid a price to live for is worth preserving and passing down to our children (both natural and spiritual), so that they can receive as a gift what costs us in time, resources, and sometimes heartache to live for.

Inheritance is not limited to material things. Inheritance also includes integrity. I want to leave a legacy of character and of faithfulness, trust, and loyalty, just to name a few. My greatest legacy I long to preserve is one of power and love that comes from a life lived from heaven's perspective. I believe that we are all divinely planned and that we were all in the heart of God with a destiny. There is a space and time where

God steps into our lives and invites us into the discovery of a higher truth about ourselves, about others, and about him. Sometimes we can find ourselves exhausted, unfulfilled, and lacking creativity, only to recognize that God is pulling us into a space of discovering more than meets the eye. The place where we can begin to address questions like "What am I here for?" and "Where am I going and who is going with me?" My real aim is that you become aware of your own value, the value of relationships, and the value of having God in your life. I want you to discover a meaningful life that is fulfilling, energized, and has purpose. A life that brings you joy even in the midst of pain and suffering. A life that is filled with light. A life lived on purpose.

I have found growing up that there are many ways of looking at ourselves and even looking at God. My hope is that you can sift through what the world tells you about yourself, about others, and even about God and discover for yourself how life lived with God and others can lead you to the life destined for you. It is my desire that some of the pivotal moments in my life will provide a spring board for you to find purpose, and the passion to live a life of destiny. As a spiritual mother, I have lived my life to make sure that the next generation has access to the treasures that have been made available to me. I have fought for the destiny and identity of my own children and my spiritual children.

When tragedy, anxiety, depression, and even suicide hits a generation like it has this one, I have made a promise to not stand by and watch it happen. I can say "Not on my watch" will I continue to allow a generation to get lost in the chaos. It is my heart's desire to see a generation rise up into the light and know who they are called to be and receive the life they were called to live. There is a place of true identity and destiny that can keep you from living a counterfeit life.

There is a life that is worth living, and no matter where you are on that journey if you picked up this book it is because you, too, are looking to become more intentional about your own life journey. I only wish that when I was your age, I had someone share with me what I am about to tell you. Most young people end up walking around in others' shadows and have yet to see the light of truth for themselves. They can end up in the dark, having to learn the hard way through their own mistakes. There are others who are intentional and willing to invest in their life from a God-given perspective. The fact that you have started reading this book indicates you are a learner and teachable. Those who are teachable become the most powerful people in the world. With a little intentionality you may just find the life you were meant to live.

> *"This will be written for the generation to come.*
> *That a people yet to be created may praise the Lord."*
>
> *Psalm 102:18, NKJV*

Section One

LIFE WITH MYSELF

WHAT AM
I HERE FOR?

Chapter 1
LIVING A LIFE OF PURPOSE

The beauty of being a young adult is that you don't have to have your whole life figured out. If we look at life as a triad, we spend the first third of it focused on ourselves (it's okay to be selfish at this stage). This is the season of your life where you can build upon who you are. You begin to embark on a career, develop new skills and relationships, and try new things. Perhaps you can find yourselves unsettled and unsure of where you are going and who it is that is going with you. Often, during this season of life, our souls are awakened, and we begin to look at living a life with purpose. This time can be very exciting if we take the time to discover who we really are. When I look back at my life after college, I can see a variety of ways without being aware of that I was actually building up in part who I am today.

One of my favorite pastimes is to go shopping. Anyone who knows me knows that shopping brings me joy. There is nothing better than going to a quaint little town and finding one of those special boutiques that carries something you haven't seen before or something that has a fresh, new design. I can usually find unique items that are native to an area. In my travels, I find that shops by the shore inspire me to want to be more relaxed and causal. When I am out West, I am inspired to connect to my earthy side and purchase jewelry that is made up of stones and décor that takes me back to nature.

When I am in the northeast of America, I find myself looking more businesslike and looking to be trendy. The one thing about boutiques is that you never know what's inside until you walk through the door and spend time discovering the treasures inside. Your life is like a boutique. It is built on what makes you special. It is native to where you live, and it is filled with all the things that make you the person you are. I use the analogy of a boutique as a way for you to access and become aware of who you are and the impact you have to those around you. Just as I love to find new places to discover in different parts of the world, there are people and places that are waiting for what you carry. Your presence, your contents, and your ability to discover your significance will be a valuable tool in learning how to serve the world around you in love. This is the greatest gift to the world.

Let's consider what your boutique might look like. Your boutique has a famous designer and has a storehouse of goods and services. It is filled up with personal skills, experiences, knowledge, other people, and has an atmosphere of its own. Your shop will grow as you build into it: new strategies, increase the inventory, add relationships, and keep the atmosphere pleasant. You will need others to keep it going. The first thing that people will notice is the name above your boutique, and that name is your given name, and your name is not given by chance. It is significant and full of meaning. God named you with purpose. Even if you didn't grow up in a God-filled home, you matter to him and so does your name. Words have power, and when your name is spoken, it is more than what people call you. It carries identity and purpose. This chapter is designed to help you see just how significant your name is to God and to your identity.

YOU ARE MORE THAN WHO YOU THINK

Today it is a struggle to know what it means to be a woman. We live in a culture that promotes success based on what we do and not on who we are. What you see on social media is most likely the woman you don't want to be, and yet being different can mean you may not fit into the norm. The truth is, we all have things that make us different. Being different makes us more beautiful, and with God's help, we can develop the strength to be content with who we are and build a life with meaning. When we are content with our uniquenesses, it becomes easier to find the confidence to try new things, to improve our skills, perform better, and have healthier relationships. The biggest confidence booster can be seeing yourself through the eyes of God and those who see you better than you see yourself.

We have used technology and social media to hide who we really are because we have the deep need to be something special. We have created an image that longs to stand out, and yet we have ignored the gift of who we really are. It's normal during this decade to try different profiles on our social media platforms to show the world our value. Perhaps we change our profile picture over and over hoping to find our best look. Sometimes older adults criticize youth for attempting to show their social media friends an image of how they want to appear to the world around them. I actually think that some of these images are simply the imagination, a dream in the heart of young people that could originate in the heart of God.

You are special to God, and he has created you in his image, full of creativity and beauty. Many times, you simply need the help of our designer to showcase who you really are. He has designed every part of you. He created you with beauty and has gifted you with what I believe is needed at this time in the world around you. You were created with purpose and value. I would like to suggest that when God had you in mind that he named you with purpose. God has placed inside of your name an original thought. You are God's original design, and he is looking for you to partner with him. Together, you can be the person that God created at the beginning.

YOUR NAME'S MEANING

God wants to show you your true self, your inner and inherent beauty. He wants to show you so that you can show the world how he intended for it to be: full of creative masterpieces living out their purposes. When we begin to see our innate beauty, we can learn how to be generous with our lives and help to make the world a better place. What if I told you that God destined you for value starting with the meaning of your name?

It is believed that ancient Hebrew people were inspired by the spirit of God to name their children. Even if people were not following God, they would receive a name for their child by the spirit of God. God loves family and inspires parents with God-given name choices, even if they are unaware of the designer. Did you know that heaven knows your name? We can see from the Word of God that God the first and ultimate Father himself created every family in heaven above and on Earth below; and every family and lineage proceeds from Father God. "From whom every family in Heaven and on earth derives its name."[1] God knows your name, and he inspired your parents to name you, as your name carries all of who you are and is infused with identity.

There is a book that shaped my life as I was learning to be a powerful woman of God. I learned about the power of the meaning of names through my friend and mentor Bethany Hicks. In her book *Own Your Assignment*, she explains that we can own who we are and live the life that God intended by first finding meaning in our names. Bethany teaches that our names can point to the future that God has for us. One of the ways we can step into our God-given assignments on earth is to see ourselves as heaven sees us.

Bethany says,

> There is a vast difference between knowing your name and owning your name. The primary distinction is that knowing is passive and owning is active. When we own our name, we are actively accepting and walking out our responsibility as defined by the name. Our names reveal our identity, destiny, and legacy, yet often our destiny will not be unlocked until we own who we are.[2]

There are times we need a wake-up call. We need a mentor, a spiritual mother to see us as God sees us, to call out our identities, and help us see into our destinies. I am indebted to Bethany Hicks for training me to own who I am by discovering the meaning of my name. What do I mean by that? I believe that my assignment in life is to know God and make him known. I have always been a spiritual person; there were just many things I didn't know about God. My assignment is to touch the world through relationships with people, so they can see what a relationship with God looks like. The meaning of my name Cathy means "pure" and my middle name, Lynn, means "lake" or "living water."

Through the discovery of the meaning of my name and inviting God into the equation, I found my purpose. I am one who speaks with purity to bring refreshment and living water to those around me. It was only in discovering that God had inspired my parents to name me with identity that my life's purpose became clearer. Discovering that the Creator of the universe cared about the choice of my name and that it carries the weight of God's intent for my life still amazes me today. You can look up the meaning of your name through many different websites. Remember, though, it is not enough to just discover the meaning of your name. You must ask God how heaven sees you. Together, with God and others, you can begin to see yourself in a whole new way.

BIBLICAL EXAMPLE

I would like to put some biblical context around the truth that God has placed meaning inside of our names. We can see from God's Word that names spoke to the destiny of people. Abram is a spiritual father in the Bible. He has an important name in biblical history, and it literally means "exalted father."[3] God made a covenant with Abram that came with a promise. He was not only a father, but God promised to make him a "father to nations." God changed his name from Abram to Abraham, in order for him to grow into his purpose. We see that God gave him a new name that not only spoke to his identity but invited him to step into his destiny.

With God's higher viewpoint, we may need to shift our own perspectives and come up higher in our estimation of ourselves. God changed his name from Abram, the "exalted father" to Abraham, the "father of nations."[4] God used the meaning of his name Abraham to speak to his destiny where he would become the father of faith who would bring salvation to all of Earth's families. Like Abram, you too may need a shift in your self-perception. God wants to shift your perspective starting with your name.

God, at times, can give us a new name that speaks to how we are seen in heaven. I remember there was a time I was learning to stand up against the darkness around me, and I sensed that God was giving me the name, "warrior." I felt that this was an invitation to grow in my ability to live in the light of God's strength, power, and love and to put on the "armor of God" to stand against the darkness. I took the name "warrior" and studied what it meant to put on the full armor of God that is found in Ephesians 6:10–17. I looked up the meaning of each piece of armor and began to dress myself as a "warrior." My perspective began to change in how I saw myself, from withdrawing to advancing even when times were hard.

There are also times where our names can come with a negative meaning. For example, the question always comes up, what about a name like Jacob that means "deceiver"? If your name has a negative meaning, allow that meaning to be redeemed by God. Let me explain. Jacob was a man in the Bible with a great destiny; he was one of the patriarchs of God's people. Yet Jacob's name means deceiver or supplanter. The story behind his name is that his mother, Rebekah, insisted he steal his older brother's blessing.

It was common that the firstborn son received a special blessing from his father. After Jacob deceived his father and stole his brothers blessing, the story doesn't end there. This was not the end of the story for Jacob! Jacob becomes conscious of his guilt and afraid of the anger of his brother Esau. It was Jacob's sensitivity to God that caused him to wrestle with God until he received a blessing that was meant for Jacob alone. His name would no longer be Jacob. From then on it was "Israel (God-wrestler); you've wrestled with God and you've come through."[5] I love how Jacob's sensitivity toward God caused him to wrestle with him until what was a negative life experience became a blessing that he could receive and give away.

Today if Jacob would ask me about his name, I would redeem the name Jacob, speak to what God did for him, and give the following God-inspired, redeemed meaning for the name Jacob: Jacob is one who is sensitive to the struggles of others and will fight for the rights and future success of those who find themselves in hard places. I see Jacob as one who is tenacious and doesn't give up until he sees others blessed!

I believe that God will take your greatest struggles and turn them into successes if you allow him to, because your name has meaning and power. It is meant to point you to your God-given destiny. If your given name speaks to a specific hardship, God wants to turn that around as you wrestle with him for the meaning and the blessing that is reserved for you in heaven through relationship with God.

MY FRIEND IRENE WHO BRINGS PEACE

The power in the meaning of a name can shift not only how we see ourselves, but how others can experience us. I would like to share with you an example. As I was writing this chapter, I spoke with an older woman who had been isolated at home for months due to the pandemic that hit our nation. I wasn't thinking about the meaning of her name. I was calling to check on her because she had just come out of surgery to repair a valve in her heart. Isolation and a pandemic can cause us to ask more meaningful questions.

I could sense that she needed some encouragement. I wanted to speak destiny into her, but I didn't want to simply say something nice; I wanted it to have the heart and power of God behind my words. Instead of the normal polite forms of communication, I decided to go a little deeper and become more authentic in expressing my heart for her. I asked her how she was doing and what she felt in her heart

God was saying to her in this season of isolation and heart surgery. This woman immediately responded with, "I think I am supposed to be around for a while, and so I just enrolled in an online school to share the hope of God with young people around me." I thought, *This woman inspires me!* This woman was widowed some years prior, just had heart surgery, was living alone, and yet she carried so much peace in a time of great distress and fear.

I was struck with the thought that in the midst of the current pandemic, even with all of the fear and uncertainty, she brought so much peace to those around her. I could see very clearly how she was still looking to be creative, and even then, at the age of seventy, she had a vision to remain generous with her life. I could tell she wasn't finished living and was determined to fulfill her destiny. I didn't know what that was specifically, so I immediately looked up the meaning of her name. *Irene* to my surprise (not really), means "peace." I dug a little deeper and found that from a biblical perspective it came from the Hebrew word *shalom*, which is in reference to the well-being of another.

All of a sudden, her destiny became very clear to me. Before our call ended, I asked her if I could pray for her. I thanked God that she was a carrier of peace and that just as I felt great peace in her presence, her future holds the promise of bringing peace into the well-being of others. She would bring about comfort, hope, and prosperity to their souls.

When I finished praying, she shared that she was touched by my encouragement and that the word *peace* meant something to her. When her husband was alive, they attended a conference called Faith-Alive in a building that had a picture of a woman name Irene who was memorialized for bringing peace to the people of that community. That was that day she learned the meaning of her name. I was able to encourage her that God wasn't done with her and that heaven sees her as one who brings peace, which is exactly what we need more of in the world today. Isn't it just like God to remind us of our identities through a simple conversation? Isn't it just like him to take something that can seem insignificant or simple, like the meaning of our names, and tie together a significant memory from the past to give us hope for a bright future?

God wants to use us to encourage others that they have purpose, often at critical times in their lives. Paying attention to the meaning of a name can bring the encouragement that is needed in a season of doubt or struggle. I truly believe that my friend Irene is exactly who the world needs today. She is one who has an innate ability to bring peace to others. I believe that if she had her own boutique named Irene that there would be a tangible aroma of peace in the air that would bring comfort, hope, and calmness to those who enter. Simply because that is what she carries as a gift to give to others. I believe that everyone who comes around my friend Irene can step into an atmosphere of peace. How God sees us can give us the ability to build our very destinies into our lives.

PRACTICAL WAY TO FIND MEANING IN A NAME

The quickest way to find the meaning of a name is to simply use a search engine to find its meaning. This is a great way to find the meaning of a name, but remember to ask God how that meaning relates to how God sees them. We can take a negative meaning and ask God how that name can be redeemed. We always want to look to God's heart, which is always to bring us back into relationship with him and his good plan and purpose for our lives.

MAKING IT REAL

Once you have your "I am" statement, begin to ask God to show you ways you can step into and own how heaven sees you. Once you see that your name has meaning and purpose, you can turn that into a declaration. For example, I wrote out my "I am" statement and started owning that I am Cathy Lynn who speaks pure words that reveal the nature of God and bring clarity and refreshment to others. Even though my words may not always be pure, I give myself the grace to grow into my heavenly identity. I am owning and growing into how heaven sees me.

This new identity continues to point to my destiny, which is to know God and make him known, to touch the world through relationship with people, so they can see what a relationship with God looks like. I can do this by the power of the meaning of my name where I continue to study the Word of God and spend time in his presence to get refreshed, so that I can refresh others with his life and truth.

You have gifts and talents, and there is a genius and craftsmanship inside you that is waiting to be developed. You really are a piece of art created by God to show the world his creative genius. His glory is being displayed through you. You are valuable, have a defined purpose, and your name carries power and destiny.

ACTIVATION

1. Research your name, and find its meaning to help you discover how God sees you. Take the meaning that you find and ask someone close to you how they see the meaning of your name as it relates to you. Then ask God how he sees you. You will be surprised at what you hear, see, feel, or have an inner knowing about. You may not hear the audible voice of God, but you can experience a sense of peace that can bring a confirmation that this is true.

2. Write out an "I am" statement. Make sure that it is loving, positive, and kind. If your name means something negative, turn it around and imagine how God could use you for good. For example, the name Heather can mean a green plant that thrives in a barren land. God might say that Heather is one who knows how to plant deep roots in dry places that go deep, where they reach water and are able to thrive.

CONCLUSION

God wants to celebrate you. He is whispering your name and calling forth your dreams. You are here for a reason and discovering who you are, and who heaven says that you are will change everything. God has given you access to your identity through the meaning of your name. You matter to God, and you matter to the world around you.

Chapter 2
LIVING A LIFE OF PASSION

WHAT MAKES MY HEART SING?

We all want to live lives that are unique and full of passion. We discover our passions in what we love to do. How many of us have said, "I love to sing" or "I love to help others" or maybe "I am really good at____?" Do you know that your passions also have purpose? They contain your gifts, talents, and the skills that you learn throughout your life. They are part of what makes your boutique unique and identify who you are. The purpose of this chapter is to discover who you are by what you love to do.

IDENTITY

We all need someone to help identify who we are and what we carry. We live in a very individualized culture that promotes self-reliance and self-discovery. Often missing from many lives is the voice of a mother or father who speak destiny into us. Many have not been raised with the loving voice of a parent who actually spoke value over them. As a mother myself, I understand that it is so easy to get caught up in tending to the needs of our children. We tend to the physical and practical, and even tend to their emotional needs by telling them we love them. Their spiritual need for significance is often misrepresented, avoided, or not considered, simply because there isn't a filter for it.

Many parents today haven't considered the power that comes from seeing our children as God sees them, from the eyes of a loving Father. Many times, religion has turned God into a far-off and distant deity to be worshipped rather than the model and blueprint for identity and destiny. Perhaps they haven't considered the etymology of a name and connected that spiritually to the heart and nature of God to bring value, meaning, and purpose as seen in the Bible. I have found that when I speak from the heart of a loving God the good qualities that I see in my own children, it touches their hearts in ways that are noticeable. I see them rise up on the inside and begin to feel loved. It causes them to see that they are seen and valued. It makes them feel significant. You may not have received the love and encouragement that helps to define and recognize your unique God-given markings, but I am here as the voice of a mother to tell you I see you, and you have value. You are loved by God and created to be a positive force of hope and life to the world around you.

I would love to help you look briefly at some key words to describe your passions, as a way of looking inside your special, cool, and chic boutique. Just as Forest Gump in the movie after his name says, "My mama always said life was like a box of chocolates. You never know what you're gonna get," so it is when people step into the boutique of your life. This mama say's they may never know what they are going to get, until they come into your presence and experience your recognizable

God markings, the things that make you, you! And life is so much sweeter with you in it, just as you are. You are more than a social media profile made up of images and stories. There are qualities and ways of measuring your value as seen in your distinct characteristics that make you the person you are today.

Let's look together at some of the qualities that might be part of what makes you the person you are. Many young people live their lives through the lens of social media, never finding the right profile. Remember, your profile is not meant to be perfect. It is meant to be authentically you, right where you are. You have to find the qualities that uniquely make up your genuine self. To help you begin the process, I will share with you some of the qualities I see in my own daughter. I invite you to take from this list any that apply to you, and add others to put a frame around the amazing person you were created to be. I encourage you to read them aloud and see which ones resonate with your heart. Here are just a few:

- Childlike adventure and joy
- Natural
- Compassionate
- Creative
- Inventive
- Fun
- Soulful
- Hard-worker
- Enthusiastic
- Friendly
- Kind
- Caring
- Courageous
- Brave
- Lovable
- Cheerful
- Long-winded (talkative)
- Clever
- Outgoing
- Hopeful
- Passionate
- Resourceful
- Self-assured
- Well-rounded

If any of these helps to define you, own them and begin to add them to your profile. Make sure you add any more of your own unique qualities that I have not mentioned. Every good gift comes from above.[1] God wants you to know how loved you are and the value you hold.

Now let's look at four different personality styles that can help you see how others are attracted to you and how you can appreciate the strength in others who are different from you.

PERSONALITY STYLES

When I was in high school and college, my peers would come to me and tell me their problems. At times, it was to get a sympathetic ear and other times to get my opinion on the matter (as if I carried some kind of special wisdom). They would say they liked being with me because I didn't judge them and I accepted them where they were. I didn't think much about my personality style back then, as we didn't have a lot of resources that talked about personality styles. I did know that I liked being with people who were more like me. I could have used some personality tools back then to help me appreciate not only myself better but also those who were very different from me.

My personality is such that I encourage others and try to look for a deeper meaning. I am also very relational. I love being with people. During this season especially, I would look to join with others where together we could try to figure out the issues in our lives. We didn't know much about life, and I didn't necessarily have a lot of wisdom back then. But I would listen, encourage, and bring strength and comfort to those around me. Together we would go on a journey into our purpose and attempt to understand our spiritualities and our contributions to the world around us. I may not have had all the right answers, but what I did have was kindness, care, acceptance, and encouragement that together we were going to get through any difficulty and that we could make the world a better place. Let me explain. When I was a senior in high school, we had a senior dinner where senior superlatives were handed out to those who displayed a high and lasting degree of success in a certain area.

These awards were given out and voted on by the entire senior class. If you were nominated for something, they kept it a secret until the winner was announced at the dinner. I was somewhat embarrassed and surprised that I received the award for "Most Popular." The reason this was so shocking is because I wasn't the head cheerleader who went out with all the guys. I didn't think I was liked by everyone. What I learned that night was that my award didn't mean I was liked by everyone; it meant that I was known by everyone. I found out that I was known for my acceptance of people. I showed kindness, care, acceptance, and encouragement.

The point is, that when we take notice of the reasons why others come around us, they can help to discover the unique qualities that mark our lives, we will see that we are made on purpose with a purpose. Your qualities mark your life and are come by God's design. They are what gives you your zeal; they are part of your passion because they are you. Did you know that when you define your good qualities you can better own who you are? It's then that you can make a difference in the world around you, and you can do it on purpose.

What do I mean by that? Have you been somewhere when somebody walks into the room, who is clearly depressed, and suddenly the atmosphere in the room becomes very heavy? It doesn't take a genius to notice someone's negative energy; it is called human discernment. You can take your good energy, something that has been clearly defined and embraced by you, and shift the atmosphere for good. We all carry at atmosphere, and you can shift an atmosphere by what you possess. Knowing what you possess is key.

PERSONALITIES AND PERSONALITY TESTS

Another practical way to find your unique self is to look at your personality. There are many personality tests that you can take, but I have a simple one that is easy and fun. You may find that there are certain aspects of your personality that you wish you could change. Your personality is something you were born with and is shaped by your upbringing, experiences, and the environment around you. How you express your personality is determined by your belief system. My hope is that you believe that God has made you and given you value.

We all have heard or felt the words of others who have defined us in certain ways. Words from a parent, a teacher, a boss, or a friend can shape the way you see yourself. For example, if you were told you are not a good student and reading is hard for you, you can come to believe that you are not a good reader, and that belief can keep you from enjoying a good book, keep you from a job you wish you had, or simply cause you to think of yourself as less than you are. When in reality, a negative report does not have to define you. You can learn new skills for reading, and you can get the help you need to learn to read.

We all have places where we can improve. Even if you are not good at something, that doesn't mean that defines you. Negative words matter to us simply because they can become part of what we believe about ourselves, simply because they came from people we trusted. Looking at some positive personality styles through a simple assessment can help shape our view of ourselves. What we believe matters because our beliefs shape our personalities and how we function in life. Our personalities affect how we will face challenges, enter society, and forge relationships.

Your personality is important, and knowing how to define yours can help you to value yourself and see the value in others. And maybe knowing your personality type can help you to appreciate yourself, like it did for me.

PERSONALITY ASSESSMENT

One of my favorite ways to assess a personality is very simple. It comes from a children's book that I used to read to my own children that helped me to appreciate their strengths. In reading it, I also learned about myself. It helped me to define my own strengths and my weaknesses, as well as define my own children's personalities and see them as individuals. I now have a filter through which to see others more clearly and not judge them because we are different. None of these assessments are meant to pigeonhole us or put labels on us. They are fun, simple ways to enjoy our differences.

This personality test has also helped me choose the people I allow to speak into my life. I have learned to choose the kind of people I need and who I want in my life. One of my best friends has strengths where I am weak. We love each other for our differences and appreciate the value we bring to the friendship. She is really good at finances and notices all the little details. She helped me do my income taxes and other financial business when I felt like giving up. I count on her a lot. She asks good questions and helps see me through some of my life's difficulties. She takes the pressure off of me to try and be someone I am not.

The name of the book is *The Treasure Tree*.[2] Seeing through the eyes of a child can spark self-recognition in a fun-loving way. It can turn on the light and become a powerful tool to help us see others in a different way and perhaps more accurately. If you are an animal lover, you will enjoy *The Treasure Tree*, as is the story of four friends depicted as different animals with four different and powerful personality traits. It is a treasure map that can lead us to understanding our nature and help us to acknowledge that different is valued. It was the winner of the ECPA Gold Medallion award for best-selling children's book of the year.[3] It can help communicate love and high value to your child.

Learning our different personality types will help us to love ourselves and others and accept and affirm our value. The story starts out with a wise old owl offering a present to all four of the best friends. The gift is a map with four great adventures that would lead them to the Treasure Tree. For these friends, the Treasure Tree was the greatest truth of all: knowing how much they loved and needed each other. The story starts out with each receiving a key to unlock one part of the way to their destination.

The friends each represent specific characteristics.

- Lance, the lion, was the leader with determination. His quick thinking helped them get across the river to the haystack where they search for golden keys to the Treasure Tree. Lions are daring and unafraid in new situations. They like to tell others what to do and are always ready to take on a challenge. They make decisions quickly and are firm and serious about what is expected.

- Giggles, the otter, likes to do all kinds of fun things; they talk a lot and tell wild stories. Giggles helped to discover the second key from its hiding place with her joyful energy and hopeful ways. Otters enjoy being in groups, and they live to perform. They are always happy and see the good in life.

- Honey, the golden retriever, was the patient one who was willing to wait to find the golden key. He took the time to listen carefully to the others, which brought about their success in finding their third key. Golden retrievers are always loyal and faithful to friends. They like to help others and feel sad when others are hurt. They are the peacemakers.

- Chewy, the beaver, paid attention to the details. He brought along his measuring tape and calculator and led them to the final key. Beavers are neat and tidy and notice all the little details. They will stick with something until it's done. They ask a lot of questions to make sure they cover all the bases. They like things done the same way, and they tend to tell things just the way they are.

With four keys in hand, these friends stand at the gate in sight of the Treasure Tree. Not knowing which key will open the gate, they put all four keys together, which made one large key that fit perfectly in the lock. They learned the important lesson that only working together will open the gate that will lead them to the greatest truth:

> *"The greatest truth you'll learn today*
> *Is friends need friends along the way."*[4]

Were you able to see yourself in one or more of these four animals? I know I could. I saw that my best friend was a beaver. I have developed over the years, but when I was younger, I was more like an otter, as I am a people-person who loves being in groups. I am usually very happy and see the cup as half full. As I started growing older, I started to see myself more like the lion. I would find myself in situations where I would be the one who would speak up first and take the lead. I also tend to be serious when it comes to a task at hand, wanting to complete it, do it well and to tell people what to do. I had to learn not to be bossy, to lead with honor, and to value others as equals and good parts of a team. You may find that, like me, you fit into two categories, as you look to identify your strengths. The goal is that we find our strengths and learn to see differences in others as strengths. Different is not meant to be separate, it is what is needed to find the perfect treasure that is just beyond the gate. The world needs you and your valued personality. There are friends who will need you to value them, so that together you can find life's treasures. Remember, you are not meant to do life alone. You just might need those with different personalities, so that together you will find the success.

PASSION

Our lives are messages. There are things that motivate you and that you have a heart for. These things are not small things. If they matter to you, they will matter to others and they matter to God. These are desires that you may have that almost always have to mature and become refined, but they are there as a force to energize your heart. Those defining qualities are there for a reason to propel you in the direction of destiny. What are you passionate about? When you can discover what brings you energy, what interests you, and makes you eager to get up in the morning you will have found your passion.

Another way to find your passion is to think about what other people come to you for. There are things that you are good at that are or will be recognized by those around you. Maybe it's math, and people come to you with help with their finances. Or perhaps you are amazing at communicating with others, and people feel comfortable around you and come to you for help. What do they want to talk to you about? What do you possess that may be a gift to another? These are all questions of self-discovery that should be answered. I believe that when you discover your passions and combine them with the purpose you find through the meaning of your name, you are well on your way to your destiny.

Remember that not every job or career path you currently travel may be one that you are passionate about. That is okay. You are building your life with skills and learning new talents. What you build into your life can be accessed later. You may be surprised when what you thought was just a summer job, actually ends up being a skill you use later in life or a way of helping someone out. Let me explain.

When I was in college I worked at a bank. I also worked in a restaurant serving as a hostess and eventually an assistant to the dining room manager. I went on to graduate college with a degree in psychology because of my love for people and human nature. Instead of pursuing that path, I ended up working as a computer programmer in a large corporation. Decades later, I was offered a position to build a café in my church where I was given the responsibility of running all aspects of this stand-alone, cash-flow business. I used the skills I learned working at the bank, in the restaurant business, and even computer programming, as I set up the entire point of sale system, which included developing menus.

My psychology degree has helped me in training, mentoring, and inspiring others to be the best they could be. All of these skills and passions ended up pointing me closer to my destiny. I was hired to not only build a café but create a space where people could connect with each other and have God-inspired conversations.

Remember that the meaning of my name pointed to my identity and destiny, which is to touch the world through relationship with people so they can see what a relationship with God looks like. This is just one more step in growing and living out of my God-given destiny. Not every skill learned was a passion of mine, but God uses everything. You are learning about yourself by defining your character qualities and looking at your personality style, all of which can help point to your God-given destiny.

MAKING IT REAL

Learning what you are passionate about will energize you and keep you moving toward all that God has for you. You will discover that you may not be liked by everyone, but you will be known for the way you express your passions. Your passions can be expressed in a hobby, recreation, entertainment, or the things that bring you joy. Make sure you find time to do those things that bring you joy, that stir your passion for life.

ACTIVATION

Answer the following questionnaire, and write this as your passion statement.

- What do I love to talk about?
- What do I never tire learning about?
- What do I do in my spare time?
- What do I dream about?
- What do I read, research, or search the internet most about?
- What are my gifts, talents, and greatest passions in life?
- Who do I have a burden to reach?
- How would I like to change the world around me?
- What do people say about me that makes my heart sing?
- My heart sings when I am _____.

CONCLUSION

We are all given one life to live. You are learning about yourself as you recognize and own what you love to do. Discover your gifts, talents, and skillset through embracing your personality. God has made you special, and he wants you to own that you are beautiful and unique, because that really matters to him. It will matter to you, and it will matter to others as they see you maturing into who God says that you are: his masterpiece. This can build the confidence you need to see yourself as loved and valued.

Above all else, remember that you are not meant to live life alone and have everything figured out. The greater truth is that friends need friends along the way, and sometimes a friend can look like a mentor or someone completely different from us. We need others who are different to help us discover the treasure that is in all of us.

Chapter 3
LIVING A LIFE OF DESTINY

WHAT AM I HERE FOR?

Why would we care about answering the question "What am I here for?" We all have been internally wired to "seek" our destinies, the place where we can leave a mark on the world. You are one of God's masterpieces who has been born into the world in a specific time with a specific mission. Your life and your passion are taking you to your destiny. There are many paths before you, and knowing which to take requires you to ask the questions: "What is destiny?" "Where am I going?" and "Who is going with me?" I would like to suggest that you are going to a God-given destiny, and God wants to go with you.

Your life is more than what happens to you; there is a purpose that has been placed inside of you by God. "Before you were born, God planned in advance your destiny and the good works you would do to fulfill it."[1] If God has planned a good life for you and this is his will, it will always be directed toward your final good. Even when life seems darkest, you can trust that God will work out all things for good for those who are called according to his purpose.[2]

FINDING THE RIGHT PATH: WHAT IS DESTINY?

Destiny is not a location, as much as it is the unfolding of the will of God over your life lived in partnership and communication with him. Your first thought might be that you don't want to give up control over your destiny, whether it is giving your life over to God or fate. God is not looking to tell you what to do. He is waiting for you to discover the good he has for you and ultimately for the good of those around you. God has given you free choice, and you get to choose your path. God has given each of us a destiny assignment. You are more than a daughter, more than a friend, and more than someone's significant other. You were born for more.

Your destiny is more than an occupation, more than the role you play in relationships and business, and more than your education. It has a God-given mission attached. Your mission will always point you to the reality of God in your life. Knowing your assignment helps you become empowered to live in your God-given destiny. Your mission will also cause you to live for more than yourself. It will take partnering with others to fulfill all of what God has given to you so freely.

God is generous with his life and invites us to live a life of generosity with him. Living a life of generosity is purposeful, passionate, and part of your destiny. When we live for more than ourselves, we find generosity is a great gift to the soul. I find no greater joy than when I give away what God has given me. I get to see it impact others for free.

40

My God-given assignment is to *connect people* to God in a way that they *become fully aware* of God, themselves, and others and that they are released into greater freedom. One of my God-given assignments was to write this book. It is one of my greatest joys to give you the gift of experience and the wisdom that has taken a lifetime to learn. I couldn't do this alone; I had to find others who could help me with my God-given assignment to write this book. I believe that God gifts us, so that we can be a gift to others.

Achieving success and making a lot of money alone never satisfies. It does feel good to give to others in some way. When we do something for someone else with no expectation of anything in return, we can find the greatest joy. You can become generous with the gifts, talents, personality, and mission that God has given you and find the life you were born for. We all know that finding a job where you benefit financially by exercising your gifts and talents is fantastic, but that doesn't mean that every job has to be a dream job. God can use every part of our lives for good when we invite him into the equation. Together you can see the unfolding of his will over your life. You were created as God's original idea to show his profound wisdom, goodness, beauty, and generosity to the world. You might just be someone who is to become the answer to what the world needs today. God has destined you for a great purpose.

WHERE ARE YOU GOING?

Where you go begins with where you are now. Learning to read the signposts along the path of your life will help to get you going in the right direction. You have come to recognize some of the signposts already; your name is significant and gives you meaning. Your identity is wrapped up in how God sees you, in your personal character qualities, your personality, and your passions. The skills you learn along the way all provide the tools needed to exercise and strengthen who you are called to be. The path to destiny is never a straight road. It is full of twists and turns, detours, and expressways. You once were on the predefined track of childhood, where you learned to follow the adults around you. Now you have the ability to discover your own path. You are going to the place called maturity, and you get to choose your destination and who will be coming along.

There was a time when I didn't want anyone telling me what to do or where to go. I wanted to create my own path. My vision wasn't broad enough. As a matter of fact, my vision was only for myself and what I wanted for my future. I spent most of my time leaning on myself and my own understanding hoping that it would provide me with a bright future. I had to look higher and discover that the dreams that were placed in my heart may just be put there by God and could be used on the path of destiny that God had created for me

The truth is that I have spent too much of my life creating my own path and being my own guide. I had never considered that God has a purpose for my life. I have done my best to plan for a life I thought I wanted to live. I became my own architect, seeking the perfect destination. Only to find that if I did finally arrive (many times I never got there because I changed destinations), it was never quite like what I had imagined. It wasn't until I had accomplished some major milestones (graduating college, getting a career, getting married, and buying a house) that something deep inside of me wanted to live for something more than my own self-fulfillment and personal needs. There was this longing in my heart to give back to the world.

DESTINY IS UNCOVERED OVER TIME

Finding meaning and purpose will take time to develop and will require God's definition. Today we are not accustomed to waiting. As much as I appreciate the speed at which we can access just about anything, I have lost the art of waiting. Waiting on God looks different than what we think waiting looks like. For most of us, waiting can seem inactive. Nothing seems to be happening. With God, waiting is where we can expect him to be doing something in regard to our growth and movement forward into destiny.

I remember in the 80s when the Polaroid instant camera became a gamechanger. The only camera I had at that time was a camera that had film that needed to be developed. I would shoot an image that was imprinted on film, and then I would have to mail the film into a photo lab and wait for the development of my photos, only to find out that many times they were too dark, too grainy, and didn't look as good as I had hoped. I would be left with real photos that captured real moments in life, the good, the bad, and sometimes the ugly. There was no redoing a selfie or even the instant deleting of a photo. The time it took to develop the film, was nothing compared to the reality of what came out in print. I did, however, learn over time how to take better pictures, how to use better lighting, and how to improve the way the images came out on print. Those prints back then were my reality. They showed the real me during real times in my life without any redos.

When the Polaroid camera came out, we got the first glimpse of instant access to our photos. Today, we have become accustomed to instant access, and we can redo and undo what we don't like. We have lost the art of development over time. We have forgotten how to accept that sometimes things turn out in ways we least expected. There is no instant delete or do over, but we can keep the good and learn from the disappointments and mistakes. Finding our destinies is similar.

The truth is the road to your destiny is more like a photo being developed in a darkroom. There are snapshots of our lives that reveal the bad and sometimes the ugly parts we go through. We may not like what comes out, and we may want to go into the darkroom and delete an image before it has been fully developed. Because of our natural tendency to rush things, this is why we need a professional developer. Professionals are patient, they trust the process, and expect a good result. Your destiny will most likely feel like it is being developed in a dark room. There is a room in the heart of God that may look dark to you, but your life is being developed with precision by the greatest professional of all.

DOT-TO-DOTS

The light really went on for me when I considered how my life is like my favorite coloring book I had as a kid, which was called a dot-to-dot book. I guess I was always looking to uncover hidden meanings or in this case hidden pictures. Humans are always looking to find meaning. We are looking to connect the dots. Do you remember when you were a kid, and you would get those dot-to-dot books? You start with dot 1 and look for dot 2 and then 3. And if dot 1 was at the top of the page and dot 2 was at the bottom, it was very tempting to try and find a dot closer and create your own picture. We can do that in life too, when we try to grow up or act more grown up than we really are. God wants to join you in the process of becoming who he says you are. He wants you to have childlike faith and enjoy the journey to your unseen destiny.

Sometimes the dots in our lives are close together and easy to find. Other times, they are far apart and across the page. I use this illustration because I have a phrase that I love to say.

We live our entire lives collecting dots along the way,
and it is God who is the one who connects them,
to the right people, the right places, and
the right things that create the image of our lives.

The truth is that we have to trust that God is making something beautiful out of our lives, even when it seems like the next dot is too far away and we can't find the connection…or when we can't find the next dot on the page at all. Life is like dot-to-dot, and God is our professional developer and the author and finisher of our life's identity portrait.

My heart is to bring dignity back to your God-given identity, so that you can grow into a powerful person who can bring honor, value, and dignity to those around you. God doesn't want to simply grow a building. God wants to grow you into a powerful person full of his nature and character, so that you can operate in love, power, and spiritual gifting that has been in the heart of God since the beginning. God wants to give you your identity not just in your first name, but ultimately with your last name becoming a child of God. God has designed your life with beauty, passion, and purpose, and he never expects you to go it alone. He longs to build a life with you that is full of heavenly treasures and riches to impact the earth, so that when others encounter you, they can see that you carry the light of God.

WHO IS GOING WITH ME?

God wants to redefine your relationship with him, so that you don't just think about him, but you actually think and act like him. We may not know everything about God, but we can know what God is like. He is a Father who is kind and forgiving, who makes us feel loved and is quick to be happy for us. God is a friend when we feel alone. God is a tall tower that protects us from storms. You may not recognize it, but God is already with you looking for you to find him. Maybe you are one who does recognize that God exists, but you don't really know him as a loving Father, a perfect companion, a guide, and a light. He is all of these and much more.

Discovering your destiny will require you to wake up spiritually. If you don't know where you are going, it's okay because you can know the one who does. I would like to suggest that God is actually walking with you right now whether you are aware of that or not. He wants you to become spiritually awake and learn how to let God define you. God wants you to join him in the dot-to-dot of your life and trust that his original design is perfect. It will take childlike faith. In a world of easy access to information and competing values and pressures, it is easy to try to figure everything out ourselves with the help of the internet. God is not looking for you to have all the answers; he is looking for you to trust and lean into him. He is looking for you to have the life that you were given. Your destiny is not so much a destination, as it is you taking responsibility to become who you were always meant to be.

DESTINY REQUIRES FAITH: WHO WILL I TRUST?

God knew you before you were ever born. God created you and the world around you and then called it good. When he was done creating, he called it "very good."[3] God gives us a glimpse of what it will take to live in God's greater mission. We can see in God's story of Abram that we looked at earlier. Abram's destiny was to become the father of faith.

Your destiny will always be attached to faith. Abram was a man in the Bible who was called by God to leave his current life and travel to the place of promise. This journey did not come without a lot of testing and internal struggles. You may not know where you are going. The thought of maturing is scary. We can read over his journey and think that it was easy for him to leave what was familiar and step into the unknown.

Destiny is always made up of one transition after another. Change almost always requires us to leave something and embrace something else. There may be some things that you are believing right now about your life that are not true. You may think that things will never work out for good. This will require shifts in your perspective and attitude. Those shifts will require you to struggle with what you believe. You may struggle with what you believe about yourself and what you believe about God. God had promised to bless Abram if he would trust him and follow him into the promise that God had over his life. He promised that Abram's name would be great, and many would follow their way to promise because of his faithfulness.[4] The problem with apprehending our own promise is that destiny requires an internal struggle. The struggle to give up our own perceptions and the step out in faith is real. This struggle will require us to believe that God has a very good plan and we can trust that we are a part of it.

The alternative is that we can do things our way and spend our lives continuing to trust ourselves. When we are divorced from the God of creation, we are left to follow our own wisdom. All too often, I hear people speak about their own spiritual awakening. The results are similar and consist of them finding their own truth. There is no absolute truth in their own thinking; they think they are only fractions of a greater whole. Their "ah ha" moment comes when they live from "their truth."

That truth is defined as anything that resonates with them. I have heard some say, "If it's true, it will resonate with me at a deep intuitive spiritual level." They never challenge what they are believing and don't like to be challenged. And to keep themselves from having to prove what is true, they say, "You don't have to be able to identify or explain it, because it is your truth."

It is easy to trust ourselves when we rely on what feels good to us. It gives us a false sense of control over our own destinies. There is no needed proof because it is just a feeling. So, what is true becomes what feels true to you. The problem with following your feelings or heart without absolute truth is that it will always lead you back to yourself and your feelings. We are emotional beings, and our emotions are God given, but we know they are also fickle. We can be up one day and down another. You were never meant to be the ultimate authority over your life. We can't control when bad things happen, nor can we control the good that happens. Good and bad will always be part of our stories, as we live in an imperfect world where bad things happen to good people.

I believe that God is calling your name and wants to walk with you throughout your life. It is time to move beyond yourself and recognize who it is that is going with you. There is a small voice that is drawing you to God. And one of the things that God is saying is "For I know the plans that I have for you, declares the Lord, plans to prosper you and not to harm you, plans to give you a hope and a future."[5] There are many plans and one purpose. That purpose begins with being united with God.

There is a spiritual bridge that connects the physical with the spiritual. We have kept Jesus in the church and allowed spirituality to become a religion. Jesus didn't just come to rescue you but to show you who you are and what you are capable of doing. And together we can all find our rightful place on Earth and bring about creative solutions and good to the world around us. You are made for more, and I believe that God wants to reset us back to his original plan.

God's heart is always to restore you and bring you out of the dark into his glorious light. God's promise is this: "You will seek Me and find Me when you search for Me with all your heart."[6] There is a greater truth for your life that will take you into your destiny, but it is not a formula to be followed. It is not a religious act or following certain rules. It is a walk with God where he turns on the light and shows you how to live "Life with me," "Life with others," and "Life with God."

CONCLUSION

"Life with me" will show you part of your purpose, starting with the meaning of your name. You can build a purposeful life with your gifts, talents, and passions. Together, with your unique personality, you can see that God has given you an assignment. As much as you want to find your mission right now, there is no assessment that you can take to show you. Your mission will come through relationship. It will take a relationship with God and relationships with others who see your life better than you see it yourself.

Right now, you are simply collecting "dots" along the way, as you discover the beautiful purpose over you. Make the best decisions you know to make, and don't try to rush the process. You don't have to connect to the "dot" closest to you, but look for the one that God has provided. God is with you and wants you to communicate with him. You will take many paths along the way to find God. God is looking to bring you to a place of identity, gifting, and beauty that is found in him, so that you live in the light and be a gift to others.

You are God's creative idea. This is what God has to say to us: "We have become His poetry, a re-created people that will fulfill the destiny he has given each of us, for we are joined to Jesus, the Anointed One. Even before we were born, God planned in advance our destiny and the good works we would do to fulfill it!"[7] God wants to re-create you to speak forth the beautiful poetry written by him. We all want our lives to reflect and be made up of good, so that we can be rewarded for doing what God wanted us to accomplish. God has put inside of you a resolve to finish the good work that he has begun in you. God will keep coming closer and closer to you until you hear him call your name and show you his love and lead you to your purpose.

My prayer for you is this:

> "I pray with great faith for you, because I'm fully convinced that the One who began this glorious work in you will faithfully continue the process of maturing you and will put His finishing touches to it until the unveiling of our Lord Jesus Christ."[8]

MAKING IT REAL

Now that you have assessed the meaning of your name and looked at your personality style, I challenge you to begin to put some of the dots together and write out a destiny statement. What are some of your character qualities, your personality, and your passions? What are some of the skills you have learned along the way that have strengthen who you are called to be? Putting all of this together, what can you see yourself becoming?

ACTIVATION

Write a statement that describes who you are.

I see that I am made for _____.

My destiny is made up of the many "dots" I am collecting through life. God has the picture of my life, and he is connecting the dots for me. Right now, my life is made up of creating an identity that looks like the way God sees me. I am choosing to act by recognizing that I was named with purpose, and my passions are God-given. They are full of life that are helping to define my destiny. Destiny awaits me, and I am beginning to get a glimpse of what that might look like.

Section Two

LIFE WITH OTHERS

WHERE AM I GOING AND WHO IS GOING WITH ME?

Chapter 4
DISCOVERING THE HIDDEN KEY TO LIVING LIFE WITH OTHERS

Living independently, stepping out, and leaving the comfort of the things you know and love and facing the world around us can be lonely and difficult, especially as a young adult. Grieving the loss of our community of relationships can cause us to question our place in the world. It can be shocking to discover that our upbringing and education did not always prepare us for life with others. We can carry hurts from the past into our present, while facing new pain that some relationships bring. How can we live with others when life gets so complicated on our own?

It took me a long time to really understand that the spiritual is connected to my mental and emotional health. God's true love and grace are intertwined and are the free gift I can not only give to myself, but one that I must give to others in order to have a healthy life. Love, grace, and mercy are all interlaced with forgiveness. It is the truest form of truth that God loves us so much that he made a way for us to become whole. If we are honest with ourselves, we will admit that we all need grace and mercy and that we have been hurt or hurt others many times unintentionally. All too often, we lean on words like *grace* and *mercy*, but we discount the very reason that we need them. We don't like the word *sin*. We choose words like "I have a problem" or "there is an issue." We want God's solution, but we have misunderstood or haven't fully acknowledged the sin part of the equation. Sin is anything that breaks God's law of love. Sin is a major disruption of God's order.[1]

We all have had to come to the revelation that God not only wants to *forgive us of sin*, he wants to *free us from the power of sin*. He wants to show us how to live in greater wholeness and freedom. God wants to freely empower us so that we live in a way that will give his love and his nature with dignity and honor to those around us.

The truth is that I want grace and mercy for myself, and I want justice for those who have wronged me. It takes learning to understand God's grace and love toward me when I expect a different response. It seems so unfair to offer grace and mercy when we have been wronged or to receive grace and mercy when we have done wrong. We must understand that "since all have sinned and are in need of the honor and glory which God bestows and receives. All are made upright in right standing with God, freely and gratuitously by His grace (His unmerited favor and mercy, through the redemption which is in Christ Jesus.)"[2] Sin always stands as the obstacle between us and God's plan for restoration.

Before I could learn to live with others, I had to learn that there are times that I miss the mark of God's perfect love. I had to not only receive God's love and forgiveness but learn to give the gift of forgiveness to myself. Receiving God's perfect love is what gave me the ability to forgive and love myself. It was only when I was able to allow God to do for me that which I couldn't do for myself, which was to love me even when I was wrong or had done wrong, that I began to understand that mercy and grace is what is needed to live with others. Walking in personal forgiveness gives me the mercy and grace to live with others.

Living in community, family, and culture is always more powerful than individual gifting and personal power. We need each other, and sometimes the people that we are in relationship with can be the most challenging. Difficult people can leave us feeling powerless, but there is a God-given principle that can save us from the heartache of feeling controlled by imperfect people. Stepping into the present requires us to let go of the things that are weighing us down from our past. The things that weigh us down I call our "baggage." The baggage we carry around doesn't belong in our present or our future. These bags are full of whatever misses the mark of God's perfect love, mercy, and grace. There is a restorative principle that has its origin in God's wisdom; it is called forgiveness, and it will help to bring us wholeness in an imperfect world.

HEALTHY RELATIONSHIPS

God's heart is always for family, and this is where we can get a first glimpse of love, as imperfect as it is. We all grew up in families that were not perfect, and many times our parents did the best they knew to do at the time. Children expect to receive love and care from their parents, but many times, hurtful remarks or comments can come from them instead. Whether or not hurtful words are intended to cause pain they may leave marks and memories that can last for a short time or for a lifetime. Sometimes the ones that are supposed to love us can seem like they are against us, and we are left with wounds that can keep us back from the fullness of who we are called to be. There are always going to be times when we didn't get the love and nurture that we needed to grow into a healthy adult. This is where we need God's mercy, grace, and forgiveness. God is love, and sometimes human love will fail us, leaving us with a skewed view of God. We can end up with thoughts about God, ourselves, and others that keep us back from the truth, the power, and the victory that awaits us.

God has a way to bring us into greater health by dealing with what is on the inside first, so that we can break out of what holds us back and break into what God has for us in the future. When we can get healthy and free, we can become the powerful women who God has created us to be. We can live the powerful lives that we were created to live, and we can become women who help others break through into greater freedom. Together we can break through into the lives that God has for us.

MY CHILDHOOD SHAME STORY

Let me give you a real-life example in my own life how a childhood experience skewed my view of God. It came when the love of God brought back a childhood memory where I needed the love and grace of my heavenly father. It happened when I was five years old. When I was a young girl, I had a best friend who was a little boy who was also five years old. We played together every day, and one day we took notice that we were not the same gender. Although it is normal to become curious about the difference between boys and girls, we decided to "see" what was so different about us. While our mothers were upstairs in the kitchen talking, we went downstairs to the garage and shut the door behind us.

The garage was empty, so we took off all of our clothes and walked around in a circle in the middle of the garage watching each other. It was like we were in a parade, and our naked bodies were the main attraction. We looked at each other stark naked and saw that we had different body parts. It was completely innocent, until the door to the garage opened and there stood at the doorway in amazement was his mother who looked at us with shock. She began to nervously tell us to put our clothes on and to come upstairs. Immediately, shame entered my innocent little five-year-old heart, and I instantly felt I had done something very wrong. I was sent upstairs where my mother was, and we both walked home to discuss what had happened. That walk home was the longest walk, as shame began to take root in my heart.

When we got home, my mother must have said something along the lines of "You can't take your clothes off with your friends, but we will talk about that when Daddy comes home." I don't remember my mother being mad, but what I do remember hearing was "wait until your daddy comes home." I was never afraid of my daddy, but now that I was carrying shame it made me feel unloved and afraid. The parents God gave to love me were now tainted with shame. Little did I know that God is likened to a father in the Bible, and that in that moment, my view of God was altered. At five years old, I decided my daddy was going to be really mad at me for doing such a shameful thing. I remember hiding behind the chair in the living room until he came home from work and walked into the front door. All I saw from behind the living room chair was his big, black, wing-tipped shoes step across the living room floor. He walked past the chair I was hiding behind and into the kitchen where my mom was cooking dinner. I sat in fear and shame, full of guilt for what I had done, which was way too much for my five-year-old heart to process. I didn't know at the time that in that moment I believed a lie about God, that God was mad at me.

My dad was really good with words and explained to me why little girls don't undress in front of little boys. He did what most parents do and told me not to do that again and sent me on my way. I didn't know at the time, that what I needed to hear from my daddy was, "I love you and I am not mad at you. You are a good little girl." This is the heart cry of every little girl, to be loved by their daddy and their mommy, because they represent the love of God to us. This incident left a mark on my heart where I developed some lies around God and lies around love.

What I needed was to know that I was loved even when I did something wrong. Isn't that what we all need, especially when we have done something wrong? We all make mistakes. Sometimes knowingly, and many times unknowingly. And there are times when those around us can unknowingly hurt us. What we need is forgiveness, so that love can flow again. The most powerful prayer on earth is the Lord's Prayer. While hanging on the cross at Calvary in agonizing pain and looking at his executioner and all those who cried out "Crucify him!" Jesus looked to heaven and said, "Father, forgive them, for they do not know what they do."[3]

These words are just as powerful today, because no matter what you have done or what has been done to you, nothing, and I mean NOTHING can separate you from the love of God. I would not be telling you the whole story if I didn't tell you the warning that goes along with God forgiving us. "But if you do not forgive others their sins, your Father will not forgive YOUR sins."[4] Forgiveness is not an option or a choice. It is something that God insists that we do. No one knows how hard this can be like Jesus, who was willing to die for the power of forgiveness to be released into our lives. When we forgive, the power of God is released into the hearts and the lives of individuals. The natural and spiritual meet to form God's perfect love. Bad spirits, called demonic forces, are neutralized, as they do not have a landing strip in our hearts to torment us with negative thoughts that produce lies. We can end up feeding these lies with our agreement that affect our thoughts and behavior. Hurt is a reality in life, but anger, judgment, hatred, and bitterness are choices. The truth is that forgiveness heals.

HIDING BEHIND MY NEED FOR LOVE

Who would have known that I could spend most of my young adult life hiding behind my need for love? As I started dating, I didn't have a good understanding of love. I ended up picking guys who I thought needed to be loved by me, as that was my way of fixing my own need for God's love. I would try to give my boyfriend what I needed. My heart needed to be cared for by the love of a man. I didn't know how to get that, so I unknowingly tried to give away the love that I actually needed myself, and that caused me to become codependent on my boyfriend and not dependent on God's love for me.

This caused me to become emotionally reliant on a guy, and I would sometimes do things to earn love that were against my core values. I called this the "Nurse Nightingale Syndrome," which got its name from the founder of modern nursing, Florence Nightingale. She organized care for wounded soldiers during a time of war. She is best known as "The Lady with a Lamp," from a phrase in a report in the *Times*:

> She is a "ministering angel" without any exaggeration in these hospitals, and as her slender form glides quietly along each corridor, every poor fellow's face softens with gratitude at the sight of her. When all the medical officers have retired for the night and silence and darkness have settled down upon those miles of prostrate sick, she may be observed alone, with a little lamp in her hand, making her solitary rounds.[5]

Nurse Nightingale had a strong desire to devote her life to the service of others and become a light of hope and healing. This is also my desire to become a light of hope and healing for others, but without the power of God's love that comes through forgiveness, I was left in the dark where shame laid buried within my heart. The Florence Nightingale metaphor that I walked in was where someone thinks they have fallen in love with someone who is broken or without the necessary skills necessary to take care of themselves. So, they need the love of a nurse to be their light and hope. I found myself choosing guys I thought I could "make better."

With God's help and my willingness to invite his light of truth into my life, he showed me that what I needed was to forgive my dad. I needed to forgive him for what happened to me when I was a child. My dad had no idea that what I needed to hear that day were the words: *I love you and I am not mad at you. You are a good little girl.* I forgave my dad and myself. For so long, I believed the lie that said trying to fix others out of love was better than receiving the love I need. Forgiveness broke that lie off of me. As I began to experience the truth of God's love for me, I began to see all the ways I had missed the mark of God's perfect love. I saw how I chose to love those who needed my love and allowed codependency to keep me from the love I needed. God's love began to heal my heart, and I became aware of the way I was looking for love in all the wrong places. Forgiveness closed the door to what held me back and opened the door to love.

If my story has triggered a memory for you, you too can receive God's grace, mercy, and forgiveness. They are available to you today. Getting healed on the inside will position us for victory on the outside. Forgiveness will not only empower you it will protect your tender heart and allow you to walk in the freedom you need to grow to become the woman God has called you to be. We all have relationships that have caused us pain. Pain can be from the small and seemingly insignificant situations to the toxic. How do we know what is toxic? Words that are offensive like "you're too fat" or "you are too skinny."

These words are degrading and cause insecurity and beliefs about ourselves, which are not true from God's perspective. Words spoken over us or to us about our physical appearance may have led to serious emotional issues like eating disorders, self-harm, and a distorted view of love. Parents are to teach their children how to love themselves, as God love's each one of us. No matter what we look like. When words mark us with pain, we need our hearts healed.

If you are in an abusive relationship or have scars that are keeping you from living fully, it is important to see a professional who can walk with you into greater healing. It is important to invite others in to get you the help you need. On the other hand, if you feel you are not living your best life because of something someone has done or said, with God's help, you can learn how to reestablish normal relationships and restore mutual respect between people of different ideas, thoughts, and beliefs. For most of us, the baggage begins at home when growing up. Our hearts had been hurt and offended by something that wasn't said or was said. This can leave an impression, a mark on us that affects how we behave. It may even impact how we see ourselves, how we see others, and ultimately how we see God. There is a place of freedom that can start with God's power of forgiveness. He can heal our hearts and allow us to see more clearly. Forgiveness can keep us from dragging around old baggage and allow us to move forward in greater freedom.

DROP THE BAGGAGE

Bringing baggage from the past will always wear you down. It is time to drop the bags. Those bags are too heavy and oftentimes too painful.

They are filled with lies and not the truth of how God sees you and loves you.

Every one of us lives life out of what we believe. Unfortunately, each of us has bags of lies that we need to let go. We can begin to do that when we understand what forgiveness is not and walk into what forgiveness really looks like. Let's take a look at what forgiveness is not.

WHAT FORGIVENESS IS NOT

It is very important to understand what forgiveness is not.

Forgiveness is not...
approval of what they did.

Forgiving another is not saying that what they did was okay. An injustice will always cause harm, even if done unintentionally. When we focus solely on the wrong, we forget that there are two parties in the equation: us and them. We cannot be responsible for another's behavior, but we must take responsibility for our own responses. When someone hurts us, we tend to only be concerned with their part. However, it is what is behind our pain, the anger, the bitterness, and the hatred in our hearts that can become just as destructive to ourselves. We can harbor hatred, anger, and any emotion that blocks love and find that we are really hurting ourselves. We can actually block the flow of love our hearts desperately need.

Forgiveness on the other hand has a boomerang effect; that is called sowing and reaping. When I forgive another, I allow the grace of God to flow back into my life. Forgiveness is the means of giving the person who hurt me to God and allowing God to deal with them. The same love, mercy, and grace that God offers us is available to them if they choose to receive it. Even if the person who hurt you is no longer alive, you can trust that God will work the same measure of grace that you give to another, into your own life.

Forgiveness is not...
forgetting what they did.

You may never forget the pain that someone caused you, but if you can give them to God and forgive them, God will cause the pain and sting to become healed. As you are healing, God may even begin to show you the pain that came into their own life that caused them to be so hurtful. Hurt people almost always hurt other people. Forgiveness is not forgetting. It is the starting point of greater freedom and healing.

Forgiveness is not...
having to let them back in your life.

When someone hurts you, you begin to build a wall around your heart to protect yourself. This wall becomes a boundary that will require refusing the person the same access until there is trust again. An offense breaks trust, and the time it took to build that trust will require us to rebuild one step at a time. This means that it's okay that some people are not permitted back into our lives until it is safe for them to be there. Learning who to let into your inner circle and who to move out to an outer circle will require you to set boundaries so that your yes means yes and your no means no. This can look like saying to someone who has hurt you, "I am sorry but I am not able to go there with you today." Learning who is safe and who is unsafe will require the counsel of a professional or at the very least a person with great wisdom.

Forgiveness is not...
the same as reconciliation.

Forgiveness is our responsibility, while reconciliation requires both parties taking responsibility for their part. Sometimes all we have to do is do our part and forgive the person, like I did with my dad, and allow God to heal our hearts. In my case, we did not have a broken relationship; I only had a broken heart, because my heart needed the love of God as a Father. Then there are other relationships that may require the other person to take responsibility for their part so that the relationship can move forward. Even when we forgive someone else, it doesn't mean that there will always be reconciliation. Reconciliation requires us owning our part, and it takes the other party owning their part. It takes two to resolve both parts, so that both can come together in a mutual agreement to move forward in relationship. Forgiveness opens the door for reconciliation where both sides can take responsibility for themselves, and the relationship is restored.

Forgiveness is not...
an option, but a necessity.

If you want to walk in wholeness and have the peace of God, you will need to forgive even if you don't feel like it. Unforgiveness can stay hidden in our thoughts and in our hearts and can affect the health of our bodies. Unforgiveness actually stays locked up inside of our whole being, and we can end up acting out in ways that are not healthy. We will either look to inflict pain on another or inflict pain on ourselves. As long as people have been hurt by another, they are chained to that hurt, and they end up carrying it around with them, even if it is packed away in the baggage that we have kept closed. We have lots of reasons why we should not forgive people. We say things like: "They don't deserve to be forgiven" or "Why should I allow them to get away with what they did?"

The truth is they don't deserve to be forgiven, and neither do we. But we can trust God and realize that when it is all said and done, no one ever gets away with anything. Mercy is a much better option. It frees us from the inward focus of our own hurt and allows the healing presence of God to restore our hearts. It gives us back our energy and allows us to drop the baggage of the past and move forward in greater wholeness. Forgiveness is not an option; it is a necessity. Now, let's look at what forgiveness is.

WHAT FORGIVENESS IS

Just as God lavishly pours out his love and grace upon our lives, we are called to show grace to others by forgiving those who truly don't deserve it. It is just as important to understand this selfish act of what forgiveness is.

Forgiveness is...
a necessary choice.

Forgiveness is a choice we make, not a feeling we have. It is never easy. When we can understand the grace that God gives us when we have done wrong, we can see how vital it is for our well-being that we pass the same grace and love to others.

Forgiveness is...
extending mercy and grace
instead of punishment.

It takes a powerful person to let someone off our hook and give them to God. It takes great strength to move past the offense and give the pain over to the only one who can bring about an unexpected healing. Grace becomes an irresistible force, as forgiveness deposits life back into our souls. When we choose to forgive, we get our power back, because we are no longer required to punish our offender. Rather, when we place them in the hands of a just God, this opens us up to a greater outpouring of love.

Forgiveness is...
letting go of our need to punish.

It is natural for us to want to see those who have hurt us punished. We have laws governing punishable offenses, which are required to keep us safe. The problem is when we find the need to take things into our own hands and punish those who have offended us. When there isn't a law for things like name-calling, condemning, holding back love, refusing to be honest, cheating us out of love, control, and manipulation, which are all wounds of the heart, we can end up holding on to anger and hatred as a way to punish others. We end up judging their wrong, while dismissing their need for grace and love, and end up reaping the consequences of those judgments into our own lives. Negative emotions become the poison that erodes love. Letting go of our need to punish, and trusting God to be their judge, frees us from the consequences of the pain that they caused.

Forgiveness is...
the key required to release the pain that weighs us
down and allows us to begin to walk in freedom.

The thing about forgiveness is that it is something that we can only do for ourselves. We can't make anybody else walk into forgiveness; it is the gift that God gives to us, so that we can forgive ourselves, as we forgive others. It is likely that you also need to forgive yourself for things you've done in the past that you are ashamed of. If you can admit them to God and yourself, you need to forgive yourself just as God forgives you. It doesn't matter how terrible the situation was in your own eyes; God wants to forgive you. Sometimes there is restitution for past sins that can be made. If so, I encourage you to do that. If it is not possible, God has forgiven you, and you need to forgive yourself and step into the grace of God. God wants you to be free and to live in the healing presence of his love, mercy, and grace.

LOVE IS A CHOICE

Love is an action verb that is shown in our ability to move toward someone, and we can do that through forgiveness, but it's our choice to forgive or not. Love cannot just be about me only; I have to learn to love God and others as I love myself. This is the greatest wisdom and greatest commandment that Jesus said when he spoke the words: "Father forgive them, for they do not know what they are doing."[6] The truth is that many have no idea that they have hurt us, or that they are hurting themselves. We are responsible to ourselves and for our actions and choices. When we walk in forgiveness, we keep love flowing in and out of our lives. This is how we live powerfully and in freedom. We have to protect our hearts and protect healthy love, and we do that by walking in forgiveness.

If there is some baggage in your life that you want to leave behind, I have a simple prayer of forgiveness that you can pray over yourself. Remember the words of God: "Be kind to one another, tenderhearted, forgiving one another, as God in Christ forgave you."[7] In order for this prayer to be effective, you will have to find the heart of God as a loving Father in these words, because just walking through a routine or ritual of prayer is the greatest way to unbelief and boredom. The most powerful prayers are those spoken from our hearts, as we move to find the love of God through his heart toward us. God loves you and is waiting for you to receive his love and forgiveness.

WHAT IF I FEEL LIKE I NEED TO FORGIVE GOD?

How many of us have felt let down by God or have been hurt by something we didn't deserve? It might sound like some of these thoughts:

God didn't stop the suffering of my loved one.
He didn't protect me when I needed it.
He allowed the abuse to continue.
He let my loved one die.

One of the biggest obstacles to believing in the power and love of God is when we experience pain and disappointment. If God is holy and perfect, why would we think it is necessary to forgive him? Wouldn't that be blasphemy? God has no sin, and we don't have the right or ability to pardon sin, but we can accuse God of many things and view God as "if" he has sinned against us, or doesn't care about us. This can lead to feelings of abandonment, fear, and lack of trust. For this reason, we must make peace with God. How we view God can be marred by or own experiences, and we can miss the fact that God promises to be with us and never leave us. Many times in the Bible, the people of God wanted to make a run for it and abandon God when trouble hit. We are told in the Bible that we will be shaken and have tribulations, but when we can live in the confidence and reality that he has overcome the world, when trouble comes, we can turn and take hold of God.[8]

There are times when we can hold on to a deep hurt that came from a time when we didn't feel that God protected us or God didn't stop a bad thing from happening. I have heard countless stories of pain, trauma, and deep sorrow where people have walked through a broken heart due to a tragic loss or have suffered a form of deep emotional or physical abuse. I have experienced my own pain at the loss of a grandchild.

When bad things happen to good people, our first reaction can be to blame God. The Bible does not teach that God is the author of pain and suffering. The Bible does, however, teach that death, suffering, and pain are the result of sin, which has its origins in a place called Eden. Sin has opened the door for evil, death, pain, and suffering as humanity continues to purposefully and deliberately turn from the perfect will of God and choose to live without God's moral structure. And what is the solution? Go back to God's original design. We will talk more about that in Section Three: Life with God. In my own pain and suffering, I had to have a heart to heart with God, because we choose the story that we tell our hearts. I had to choose to say that I don't understand why death and loss happened to my children who follow after God, and I may never understand the fullness of it here on Earth, but I choose to believe:

> *"Yet I am confident I will see the Lord's goodness*
> *while I am here in the land of the living.*
>
> *Wait patiently for the Lord.*
> *Be brave and courageous.*
> *Yes, wait patiently for the Lord."*
>
> *Psalm 27:13–14, NLT*

God is calling us back to the place where we can live in the light of his presence and rebuild the places in our lives that have been destroyed, hurt, abandoned, or are hopeless. God wants us to live in the light of his love, and he has provided the way through the power of forgiveness.

MAKING IT REAL

A PRAYER TO FORGIVE OTHERS

You may need to write this prayer down and then rip it up if this is too painful to speak out loud to God. Or you can place the person who you need to forgive in front of you and begin to say,

> I want you to know _____ (put in the person's name) that I forgive you. (It's that simple). I choose to let go of the pain, the hurt, and all the ways I have held on to this offense.

You may experience a lifting or other sensation, or you may feel nothing at all, but there is power in these words, and God's grace is setting you free. Then speak the words back to God:

> I receive today a healed heart and ask that you fill me with the love you have for me, so that I can love others freely. In the name of the one who made forgiveness possible. In Jesus's name, amen.

This prayer has the power of God on it. You may now be feeling a sense of freedom, lightness as the actual fabric of your being changes. Instead of tension and pain, you may be feeling peace and hope. Before we leave the power of forgiving others, you may need to forgive yourself for something you have done. This can be the most humbling part, to admit that we have been the cause of pain in another or even in ourselves because of what we had come to believe or because we drew the wrong conclusion. If you need to forgive yourself, you can choose to do that today. This prayer will shift the atmosphere of your heart if you choose to believe in the power of God to forgive you.

A PRAYER TO FORGIVE MYSELF

> I want you to say out loud, God, as I have forgiven others, I want to give myself a gift of my own forgiveness. Speak your own name out loud. It is important to hear you speak your name because it makes it very personal and real. For example, I would say, "Today I choose to forgive you, Cathy." Today I choose to forgive myself for _____ (fill in the blank). I let it go and forgive myself. I will stop punishing myself because you accept me right where I am. Help me to love myself, as you love me. In Jesus's name, amen.

There is tremendous power in these forgiveness prayers, because they are based on the mercy, grace, and love of God. They can make your life a whole lot easier. If you have faith to receive this truth, I want you to declare over yourself right now, "I am free, I am valued, and I am loved!" You are becoming a powerful woman of destiny.

MOVING BEYOND FORGIVENESS INTO ACTION STEPS

I have five steps that God has taught me to walk out forgiveness. I know there are many more that you and God can develop for your own personal situations. Here are the steps that have helped me to move forward:

1. ## Manage your thoughts and your words

    Allow the words you speak to yourself to be seasoned with truth and what God has promised. You are forgiven. You are loved, and God is helping you to live in greater wholeness. Do not allow the words you speak to yourself simply be what you are feeling. Put the pause button on any negative thinking, and look for the truth. Stop saying things like "Nothing is going change," "I don't know if I am going to be okay," or "Nobody cares about me." God doesn't shut the mouths of our enemies or silence their words, but he will put his words in our hearts and teach us how to use them as weapons. Remember, to manage means to take charge or be in charge, to rule over, and to organize. Take charge of your life. Become your own manager and follow after God.

2. ## Connection

    Find a community of people you can grow with. If you need professional help, reach out today and get the help you need. Find a place where you have safe people who know you and love you and see you better than you see yourself. A place where those around you have a bigger view than your small part. Together, you can grow into maturity.

3. ## Communication

    Get the courage you need to have those tough conversations. Get the help of a counselor, mentor, or friend. Many times, the conversations we try to avoid are the very topics of conversation or areas that need to be addressed, so that we can have hope of a better future. It is our basic human nature to always think the worst first, but when we are honest and tell others what we need, we can find a way forward. It's time to speak up and let those who matter know what you need.

4. Work on Boundaries

Most of us did not grow up with healthy boundaries. Children are not born with boundaries. If you need help with boundaries, find a mentor, coach, or counselor to help you develop healthy boundaries. Clear boundaries give you a well-defined sense of who you are, what you are responsible for, and the ability to choose.

5. Face your problems and move toward fixing them

Admit what the problem is and take action to get the help you need. Start today and reach out to someone who can help you reach your goal. We are not self-made, and we usually need help from the outside. If the path you are on is the wrong path, make adjustments and be humble and flexible to ask for directions.

6. Conclusion

God wants you to be reconciled back to his love, so that you can learn to love others as yourself. Forgiveness is more than a principle; it is the power to free us from the sin or the things that so easily entangles us. We all want justice for those who have hurt us and mercy for ourselves. Forgiveness doesn't mean forgetting; it means releasing those who have hurt us to God and giving God the right to judge. God wants justice and mercy for all. If we let our walls down and ask for forgiveness, we can let God protect us and empower us to live in love. This is what it means to live in the light of God's love, and it will help us when life with others becomes difficult.

Chapter 5
A STRONG MIND

HOW I THINK IS IMPORTANT

A. W. Tozer said, "What comes into our minds when we think about God is the most important thing about us."[1] What we think about ourselves is also really important. It becomes the filter through which we view ourselves and the world around us. I don't know about you, but I have spent a good part of my life allowing what others have said about me determine how I see myself. When I do this, my thinking gets me in trouble. I have learned that there is a voice that is the voice of God, and that voice always thinks of me as better than I think of myself. There is a voice that comes from God that encourages, strengthens, and brings comfort. The first place I believe where our thinking goes astray is in how we think about ourselves.

Right thinking will keep us from thinking more of ourselves than we ought, or thinking too little of ourselves. Many of my opinions about myself came from those comments I had heard spoken or came from my family traditions. All these things that I read and experienced built my belief system. As I grew up, I came to realize there are many things I believed that simply were not truth. The reason this is important is because what I think influences how I will act. This is especially true when it comes to what I think about myself. Let me give you an example.

CHATTY CATHY

Have you ever been given a nickname or been labeled? The old adage "Sticks and stones may break my bones, but names will never hurt me" is simply not true. I grew up being called "Chatty Cathy" by my family. Sometimes even enduring names or labels that are placed on us can create a false belief about ourselves. We all are born into imperfect families, and even poking fun at each other can cause us to disregard ourselves. The very people who are meant to love us and build us up, until we can stand on our own two feet, can attempt to be fun loving and use teasing as a way of affection until one day we realize that we have come to believe something that is not fully the truth.

As we grow up, we soon become aware of our own brokenness. We all have things that we are believing about ourselves that are not true. We end up taking into our adult lives habits, patterns of thinking, and the beliefs of our parents and not even question if they are all true. How many have come to believe what their parents have said about them? If it is positive, that can be a good thing that challenges us to see ourselves better than we alone see ourselves. Sometimes teasing and labels can have a negative connotation and end up holding us hostage to something that is not even true. We then begin to feel that way about ourselves.

For example, I grew up talking a lot. It's funny how certain words spoken over us as a child and certain images stick in our minds and can become a blessing or a curse. I was born in 1959, and the toy company Mattel manufactured a doll from 1959 to 1965 called the "Chatty Cathy" doll. This doll was on the market for six years and was the second most popular doll of the 60s, with Barbie being number one. I wasn't named after this doll at my birth, but I certainly seemed to inherit the meaning of her name as a child. There is meaning in our name, as we discovered earlier, and there's also meaning in the names that people give us. Sometimes it's good for us, and sometimes it can be to our detriment. In the case of Chatty Cathy, I grew up thinking that talking too much was bad. To reinforce that belief, I often got on my grade-school report card a check under the boxes for good and bad behavior. My report card often had the box "talks too much" checked. I was told over and over that I had to learn to save my talking for after school.

As I grew, I associated my talking with bad behavior. Then into my adult life, I often felt embarrassed when I thought I spoke too much. I began to think that people didn't want to hear what I had to say. The truth was I did need to mature and learn when it was okay to talk and when it was important to listen, but I also needed to see myself from God's perspective and how he created me. The personality we start out with in childhood is our God gift. It just needs to mature. With the right amount of love and training, we can take what appears to be bad behavior and turn it into something good. And if we didn't get that growing up, God has a way of taking the words or labels that have hurt us and turning them around to bless us.

That happened to me just recently when a man who I didn't even know spoke words of encouragement over me. He had no idea of how I was labeled, knew nothing about my childhood report cards, nor my negative self-talk that agreed that "I talked too much." He said, "I don't know if you are familiar with the doll Chatty Cathy? But I know that many have used that term in a negative way, but I see that you have the ability to speak to others in a way that comes with influence and authority. When you speak people listen." Wow, was that a shift in perspective! Here was this man I didn't even know until that day being used by God to highlight how God saw me and disempower the negative label that I had come into agreement with. God was inviting me to see myself as he sees me and replacing the lie that I had come to believe about myself. God is always looking for our agreement with how he sees us, so that we can think like him. It was easy for me to believe what this man had said to me, because it came through a filter that reminded me of God, with so much love. God can use other people to give us the strength to see ourselves differently to bring about a positive change in our lives.

THE BATTLE OF OUR MINDS

Any opinion or description that is not grounded in the way that God sees us or wants us to see ourselves is based on a lie, because God *is* truth. Lies get lodged in our minds and form toxic thinking that steals our joy and can steal our identities. God wants to reboot our belief system and give us his truth. He doesn't want us to fear the words of others. God wants us to have his words, his mind, so that we can have the courage, strength, and comfort we need to battle the lies. God makes it clear in his Word how taking care of our inner world will lead us to health. Soul care is a common term, but most don't understand that caring for ourselves is significant to God. God wants us to move beyond how we think, into how he thinks about us.

When I allowed "Chatty Cathy" to define me as someone whose talking caused bad behavior, my self-image and how I felt about myself was not good. My thoughts caused me to choose to keep quiet when my talking could have been beneficial. My negative emotions were pointing to something. I needed to find out the truth. The words of a stranger were used to encourage and strengthen me with the truth of how God saw me. God's version of a Chatty Cathy is someone who speaks and people listen. This battle over our minds is over the way we think, the way we feel, and the choices we make. Words, labels, and comments spoken over us are all looking for our agreement so they can "land" or "stick." There is power in agreement. We can either agree with what God says, that comes through a filter of love, or agree with what others have said about us. If we agree that we are not good enough, we give power to this belief, and it becomes our truth even when others see us differently. Finding out what God has to say about us is really important.

WHAT GOD SAYS ABOUT US

Sometimes there are arrows of lies that get stuck in our hearts. The only way to get them out is to find those who love us enough to tell us the truth. Sometimes that looks like God speaking to our hearts, and other times we can ask those we trust and who see us better than we see ourselves to speak into our lives. Ultimately, it comes down to God who will speak to us and show us the truth of how he sees us. The secret is to learn that the lying voices are not you. Just because you picked them up (heard or felt them), doesn't mean it's you. How do I determine if those words are not mine to carry? By learning to hear the truth of how God sees you and ultimately learning to hear the voice of God, which we will talk about in another chapter. Let's destroy some of those lies now by receiving the way God sees us!

Here are a few truths that God has spoken to help you get started:

I am accepted. God's love always accepts you as you are and draws you by his grace into who you are supposed to be in him. "But those who embraced Him and took hold of his name were given authority to become children of God."[2]

I am secure. "If God is for us, who can be against us? [3]

I am significant. God created us for significance. "We have become His poetry, a re-created people that will fulfill the destiny he has given each of us, for we are joined to Jesus, the Anointed One. Even before we were born, God planned in advance our destiny and the good works, we would do to fulfill it!!"[4]

I invite you to say to God:

> *God, I ask you to reveal to me any area in my life where I have believed a lie about myself. Any place where I have agreed with a lie and have believed the lies of the enemy as the voice of truth. I ask that you break the power of that voice and rewire my thinking so that I can see how you see me and so that I can feel how you feel about me. Let your voice become the only voice I hear right now. Amen.*

OUR PLACE OF PROMISE

God has a place of promise for each one of us to live in. This place is the spiritual reality of a Kingdom other than this world. It is called the Kingdom of God, and this is the spiritual realm where God resides. The language that is used is significant, because a Kingdom is a realm associated with a ruling power. God's ruling power is always love. The promise is that we could find our place in God through the landscape of his Son. The real question when talking about the landscape of God's Son, is "Who is Jesus?" Everything written about God in the Bible is to point to the person of Jesus, so that we can become like him to the world around us. God gave us the promise of making things right by giving us the gift of his Son who came to put us back into right relationship with God and to make us the whole person that God created from the beginning. Jesus also came to model what living in our humanness looks like. He came to teach us what true love is. Loving God, loving ourselves, and learning how to serve in love those who God brings our way. In this way, we too can become a gift to the world around us and show them what living in a spiritual reality looks like.

We were never meant to become a god ourselves. We were never meant to find our small piece of God from out in the universe somewhere. We were created by the God who reigns above the universe to learn to live in closeness to him. Jesus didn't just die for our sins; he died for our humanness. All of our total personhood that not only contains our spirit, but makes up our minds, emotions, feelings, and our physiology. Jesus died for humanity, so that we could once again be compassionate, understandable, approachable, and accessible. This Jesus came to show us what it means to be human in a broken world. Jesus died to show us how to live with God, live with ourselves, and how to live with others in love, respect, and honor.

The promise is to become like Jesus. Jesus is the exact representation of God and the model of how we were created to be. To be more like Jesus is to be more like God. We were all created in the image of God.

So, who is Jesus? Most religions will acknowledge that Jesus was a prophet or a good teacher. They agree that he was a godly man. Other religions have their own prophets or godly teachers who they believe are equivalent to Jesus.

Here we need to be clear. There will never be anyone else, other than Jesus, who could pay the penalty for humanity's sin and die once and for all. He is the only one to provide the way to wholeness and reconcile us to the Father. Jesus came to represent our humanness and conquer sin. "He understands humanity, for as a Man, our magnificent King-Priest was tempted in every way just as we are, and conquered sin."[5] Jesus is the promise that we could find our place in God through the landscape of his life.

Jesus always speaks of himself in relationship to God, who he calls Father. Their relationship becomes the model for us to live in relationship with God. Jesus also said that "I and the Father are one."[6] This word is not meant to be *singularity*; it means "unity" or "agreement."[7] Jesus and God are in union and complete agreement.

Jesus and God are one, and we all need Jesus to show us our place in God's heart. Sometimes God will use a stranger who has renewed his thinking to speak to us from the heart of God to change the way we think about ourselves. Just like that man spoke to me who took an old negative label and turned it into an empowering identity statement. One of the ways I seek to invite people into a new way of thinking about themselves is to do like Jesus and serve others in love. I do this when I am in a restaurant. When a server comes to serve me, I choose to serve them in love by asking them their name. I do this to honor them, but I also love to bring heavenly identity to them by looking up the meaning. I take out my phone, Google their name, and ask God how he sees them. When they come back with my food, I have already put together that meaning in a brief statement that speaks encouragement and strength and sometimes comfort to them as I give them a word of affirmation.

I was just in a restaurant the other day, and my server's name was Cheyenne. When I looked up the meaning of her name, it said "unintelligible." At first, I thought that it wasn't very honoring. So I asked God how the meaning of Cheyenne could become a gift to her. I immediately got the impression that she was a young woman who had a heart for the disenfranchised and those whom the world can overlook, as not being smart enough. That she would bring hope and respect to these kinds of people. I gave her the gift of an affirmation of how God sees her. We can make affirmations about ourselves and try to build ourselves up, but it is always more powerful when someone else gives us the gift of affirmation. The word *affirm* means to give strength to someone.

I believe God wanted to invite Cheyenne into a promise over her life, and immediately she said, "That makes sense because I do that in my life."

Her whole body seemed to smile, as she walked away having stepped into a new way of thinking, if only for a moment. True spirituality is not about ascending into the heavens or connecting to the universe; it's about being human and learning to see ourselves as God sees us. It is about learning to love and serve others like Jesus did.

I believe that God is raising up powerful young women (and men) who will learn to walk in the truth and ways of God and be used to help others overcome their negative thinking about themselves. They will overcome fear, anxiety, guilt, and pride that have plagued a generation with depression, self-hatred, insecurity, and suicide. It will take learning how God thinks and spiritual leaders, mentors, and spiritual mothers and fathers to teach you how to war against those things that are looking to take out a generation. You have a choice of who will rule over you and how you will live. You can settle for what has been said about you, or you can look for the truth. It's time to own who you are in God's eyes, and that will take addressing those things that stand in the way.

INTERNAL GIANTS

One of the ways I learned to change my thinking was through facing my internal giants. I have had my own giants to overcome. My greatest giant was feeling like I was not being good enough for other people. My giant's name was People Pleasing. I would like to share with you how I learned to conquer this giant. This was one of the most difficult years in my walk of faith. I had been walking with God for sixteen years, and I had done a lot of things for God in the area of ministry. It appeared that I had it all together and was a born leader. The problem was that what I saw in myself did not line up with how God saw me. God wanted me to conquer the giant and love him more than the love of looking good in front of others. If I wanted people to see God in me, there were some things that had to get out of the way. Sometimes God has to strip us down of all the things we put on ourselves to appear better than we really are on the inside, to build us back up stronger. The most painful part is that I had no idea what I really thought about myself. I needed to hear from God his truth, to stop performing for others. I didn't know what was coming, and I was completely taken off guard, or better said, my guards were taken down.

I had built myself up in ministry, and things were looking really good. That happens when you are caught in a performance trap. What I didn't know about myself was that I really cared more about whether I was looking good and pleasing the people in front of me than I cared about becoming like Jesus. I started to think of myself as being better than I really was at that time in my life. I had thought I was a humble person, but I really had learned to mask my pride and was walking in false humility. False humility where I became easily offended, rather than being quick to listen to see the other side and slow to respond. I enjoyed judging other people, not realizing that I had to get the log out of my own eye before I ever could address the speck in another's. I was preoccupied with self, where a humble person is just as deliberately attentive to others as to himself. My pride had gotten the best of me, and I had to learn that my preoccupation with myself needed to be balanced with how God saw me more than how others saw me.

At the beginning of March 2002, I was teaching at a community Bible study. I had been a part of this ministry for many years. I had gifts from God that I wanted nothing more than to use for God and be something special. It was toward the end of my time in this ministry that God answered a prayer of my heart in a way that I didn't expect. I had asked God to make me more like Jesus, while on the inside I didn't know that I had some character issues that needed to be addressed. I had a need to live for the approval of others, always looking for affirmation from them. This caused me to be driven by the need to be successful and run ahead of myself and run ahead of God. I expected myself to look good to others and was never able to be good enough. The truth was that pleasing God looks very different than trying to please others, including myself.

I hid behind my leadership role in false humility, and as I did, God allowed me to face the truth about myself. I also was hiding behind my own insecurity. It was the last teaching I would give in that season until God healed my heart. I stood before a room full of women, where I suddenly had a spiritual experience like none before. This experience so humbled me that I could hardly get through my teaching. As I began to speak, I immediately became aware of the words that I was speaking. These were words I had written to teach the women, but deep down I was looking to impress them. I began to speak, and as I did, my words felt very heavy, and I was slow to form them, as if I had peanut butter stuck to the top of my mouth. As I watched the words try to come out of my mouth, I started to feel the humiliation of not being able to speak well. Ironically, if I really was humble, I wouldn't have been able to be humiliated. God can, and often does, humble the prideful.

Humiliation started to fill my soul. I then looked out at the women and thought, *They are all going to see that I am a mess.* Then the second revelation hit. God allowed me to come face-to-face with the reality of who I was and who I wanted to be. I felt like I was two different people. I saw myself on one side as a woman who loved (feared) God, and I also saw myself on the other side as a woman who feared the reactions of the women in the audience. I became aware that I was double-minded.

One part of me wanted to look good in front of people above anything else, and the other part loved and wanted to serve God and other people in love. I couldn't have it both ways. I could either continue to live to please man (or women in this case), or I could live to please him. I love the fact that when we love God, he reveals our weaknesses in a way that comes not only with a solution, but he does it in a way that only we know it's God. All of this took place internally. No one had any idea what was really going on inside of me that day. I went home hiding my humiliation and actually was so affected by this experience that when I got there, I fell to the ground and cried out to God. "I am broken, and I can't fix myself." As I poured my broken heart out to him, he came to me and began to still my heart with his love.

MY HEALING PROCESS

After encountering the truth of myself through the love of God, I knew I needed to step down from my leadership role for a season to renew my mind and heal my soul. I spent three years learning about the love of God and his promises. I got around those who were ahead of me on the journey and allowed them into my inner thought life. I began to learn what was true about myself and what was a lie. I began to learn what was wrong in my life and what was the right way to live. I found a community of people who were willing to walk with me into greater truth. I also started attending a church that taught on the transformation of the inner man/woman. It is never wise to "dig in your own garden" and look for the weeds in your soul. Inviting God into the process always brings truth. Walking with others who have walked in truth and have a proven history of a healthy soul, always provide wise counsel. And if need be, seeing a good counselor will bring healing to the soul.

During this season, God had to trim back my gifts for a year to heal me and work on my character. There is one thing worth living for and giving your all to and that is to see God as he really is and to see ourselves as God sees us. To live with a healthy soul will take courage to walk in full disclosure with God and some trusted people who we can share our struggles with. We need God, and we need other people to grow in health.

MAKING IT REAL

If you are willing, this is a bold prayer to invite God to go deep beneath the surface to your inner thoughts and motives that nobody else can see. This is a powerful prayer, as God will begin to show you things that need to change to bring you into health from the inside out.

I invite you to pray the prayer of Psalm 139:23–24:

> *"God, I invite your searching gaze into my heart.*
> *Examine me through and through;*
> *find out everything that may be hidden within me.*
> *Put me to the test and sift through all my anxious cares.*
> *See if there is any path of pain I'm walking on,*
> *and lead me back to your glorious, everlasting way—*
> *the path that brings me back to you."* [8] *Amen.*

ACTIVATION

Reflect on these questions:

1. What have I attempted to justify for some time?

2. What are others trying to tell me?

3. Ask God, how have you shown me your love that was overlaid by my own lies?

If need be, get around others who see you better than you see yourself, and invite them into this process. Find a mentor, spiritual mother or father, or leader to help you see yourself as God sees you.

CONCLUSION

What we think about ourselves is really important. When we allow the truth of God and others to challenge how we think, we can grow our souls. I am the only one who can be responsible for what I put into my mind. I can allow God and others to help me grow into the likeness of Jesus, but it will require me to learn to grow up and face my fears and invite God and others into the process. I am created to live life with others. God wants me to be powerful and to be who I am created to be. I will live my life on purpose, because I am beginning to understand myself better. God has a destination point, and I am moving toward that.

Section Three

LIFE WITH GOD

AM I REALLY PART OF SOMETHING LARGER?

Chapter 6
WHO IS GOD REALLY?

Knowing God well enough is to say yes to living in the light in the midst of a chaotic world where the light seems to have been turned off.

INTRODUCTION

I sit writing this chapter during Christmas week. I am reminded of all the Christmas songs and the joy that this season brings. I still remember the Christmas story being told from *A Charlie Brown Christmas* that played every year during this time. Charlie Brown asked his best friend Linus the true meaning of Christmas. Linus, the most insecure of Charlie Brown's friends, is the one who steps forward and pronounces to Charlie what Christmas is all about. I love how God deliberately chooses those who the culture overlooks to become the brightest lights. He chooses those who the world wouldn't expect, to make clear his message.

And there were in the same country shepherds abiding
in the field, keeping watch over their flocks by night.
And, lo, the angel of the Lord came upon them, and
the glory of the Lord shone round about them: and they
were sore afraid. And the angel said unto them, Fear
not: for, behold, I bring you good tidings of great joy,
which shall be to all people. For unto you is born this
day in the city of David a Savior, which is Christ the
Lord. And this shall be a sign unto you; Ye shall find the
babe wrapped in swaddling clothes, lying in a manger.
And suddenly there was with the angel a multitude
of the heavenly host praising God, and saying, Glory
to God in the highest, and on Earth peace, good will
toward men.[1]

I always wondered about things like the glory of God showing up. I
had envisioned the greatest light known to man shining and looking
like an aura that you would see above an angel. I honestly ignored the
fact that the people present when the angel of the Lord showed up
became afraid. I thought it would be really cool to see the bright light
of God or an aura, but the truth is that with a true encounter with God
comes with it a sense of a reverential awe of his majesty. I never saw
God's holiness in it. I rather liked the good feeling when I heard "good
tidings of great joy." After all, it's what Christmas is all about, right? I
never considered the truth that God is good, and God is holy. I didn't
consider that the spiritual realm of angels could cause a reverential fear,
but they absolutely do.

It bothered me when I heard people say they saw angels and that they
are cute, or they are their best friends. It just didn't sound right. What
is the truth about angels? There are countless encounters with angels in
the Bible where the first thing they say is "Fear not!" I understand that

any paranormal experience would cause a natural response of fear, but I also believe that with an angelic encounter comes an awareness of the love and reverential presence of God.

Angels have many functions in the Bible. Some of which are, worship around the throne of God[2] or protection from danger. We see that God sends his angel to deliver three men out of a fire[3] or to communicate a message like when an angel comes to Mary to announce that God has found great favor with her and that she will conceive a Son and call his name Jesus.[4] There are other angelic functions, but the one I want to share with you is my own experience with an angel.

ANGELIC ENCOUNTER

My seventeen-year-old daughter had gotten in a very serious car accident. The car she was driving hit a very sharp turn on a road in the woods near our home. She was driving too fast. We had lived in a rural area with a lot of woods and windy roads. I received the call from the police and headed directly over to the scene of the accident to find a fire truck, an ambulance, and police cars all with sirens and lights flashing. They wouldn't let me into the ambulance, where my daughter was strapped down on a board getting stabilized to safely make the drive to the hospital. I walked, dazed, over to where the car was lying overturned in the woods. I looked over in horror to see her vehicle flipped upside down. It was crushed at the windshield and various other parts. I stood in disbelief.

Then something else caught my attention. There was a huge tree directly in front of her car that she missed by just a few inches. If the car had gone a little to the left, she would have been in a head-on collision and would have most likely lost her life. Then I looked down at the ground. There was what appeared to be a tree stump left in the woods. It was as if someone had randomly cut down the tree at some point and had just left the stump. I realized that this stump was probably what caused the back tire of my daughter's car to get stuck, and stop quickly, which then caused the car to flip to its current position, missing the tree in front only by a few inches.

I followed the ambulance to the hospital, and I asked God to spare her life. Once inside the ER, I had a moment when the doctor rushed out to grab something, I laid my hands on her body and said these words: "Be healed in the name of Jesus. No internal damage." She was rushed off for x-rays where it was determined a miracle had taken place. Nothing was broken, and there was no internal damage. The doctor looked over to me and said, "Someone was looking out for her; she was a very lucky girl!"

A few days later while in worship, I opened my heart in vulnerability to God. It was when I was laying my heart raw and bare before him that I encountered my first and only angel. I placed my fear, my traumatic emotions all on God, and in a quiet way I could feel my heart thanking God for saving my daughter. It was a heart-to-heart connection with God. Suddenly, in my mind's eye, or what I call my divine imagination, I saw what appeared to be a huge warring angel. It stood about thirty feet tall and was dressed in metal armor holding a sword and was standing next to the tree in the woods where my daughter's accident happened.

As soon as I got a glimpse into the spiritual realm where this angel dwelt, my body was struck with fear. I started wailing and crying, as my whole body shook. One of the pastors came over and asked if I was okay. I did everything I could to say, "I just saw an angel." The appearance of this angel not only caused me great fear but came with a reverential knowing that in God's great love, He had sent forth an angel to protect my daughter. I had never seen this kind of love. It was these words that became my reality: "For He shall give His angels charge over you, to keep you in all your ways."[5] And these words: "The angel of the Lord encamps around those who fear Him and rescues them."[6] This was not an encounter with cute little angels who had become my friends; this was an authentic encounter with the awesomeness of God.

Today more than ever we need to know the truth about God. God is a mystery. We may not be able to know everything about God, but we can know the truth of his nature, character and his Word. As the world appears to grow darker and darker, people need to have hope. They need to know that God is with them. The world is full of natural disasters, personal disasters, and emotional turmoil that are destroying humanity. It's easy to start to question that if God were real, why would he allow bad things to happen? This would be easy to do if we weren't aware of how things were at the beginning when God created the world and what happened to make it so bad.

Darkness can be debilitating and filled with bad news. We live in a world where pain, suffering, and pandemics can leave us wondering if there really is a God. Like Charlie Brown, we can wonder if there is really great joy to be had in our lifetime. Does anyone have any good news? Hatred, racism, political unrest, and warring against each other can leave us hopeless. We are told that "He who hates his brother/sister is in darkness and walks in darkness, and does not know where he is going, because the darkness has blinded his eyes."[7] Hatred and pain have a way of blinding us to the reality that all people have value and are formed in the image of God.

We are all apart of living in a world that has fallen from God's original design and have lost the reality of the light that dwelt with us. When darkness comes, it brings with it fear, anxiety, depression, and loneliness. We all would like an angelic encounter, but what we really need is God who is light and in him is no darkness at all.[8] We need more than an angelic encounter; we need to understand what causes a multitude of angels to sing, "Glory to God in the highest, and on earth peace, goodwill toward men."[9]

THE REALM OF THE SPIRITUAL

Today, many young people are looking for a form of spirituality to light their way to God. They wonder if there is a God, and if so, what is he like? Is he the god of the Christians, the god of the universe, the God of all religions? This is normal and good and part of the growth process. I believe that we all have to come to a place where we either take off the coat of religion that was put on us and put on our own spiritual coat. My heart is to help those who have not found their own spiritual covering. Many religions have writings and a book to define their gods. Many different spiritual paths have made their way onto American soil.

When I was growing up, the spiritual path in front of me was Christianity. This is the one I know best and have personally experienced as the true light of the world. I spent my college years studying different religions in an attempt to uncover the mystery of God. Although I grew up in a Christian household, I was biblically illiterate at that time. I did not know the God of my faith and had only adopted the Christian way of life. It has taken me my lifetime to get to know God, and yet I only know him in part. God is a mystery, and it has been my greatest joy to step into the unknown and learn, experience, and continue to get to know this God.

There is a spiritual realm that is, for the most part, unknown. My goal is to awaken you to the reality of getting closer to God and help you discover the ancient path to a life with God that was laid down over two thousand years ago. I believe that our stories can inspire and awaken others on their journeys to finding God. I have lived long enough and investigated enough religions to know that what I am sharing with you is the truth. I will not just share *my truth*; I will give you biblical references that have stood the test of time. If I am wrong, I will spend the rest of my life making it right. When I found God, it was only because God had already found me. God found me as a child, but when fear took hold of me, I turned off my sensitivity to him.

I did go to church as a child, but it was more like school than anything else. God did find me again at home alone right after college. It was just like any other day where I was living the life I thought I was supposed to live. There was no crisis, sickness, or death in my family that caused my spiritual awakening. Rather, it was this aching in my heart that seemed to always be there. It was the sense that there had to be more to life that awakened me. It was this deep feeling in my soul that everything that I was living for was not satisfying the longings of my heart. The truth was I didn't even know what that was. I simply wanted to know if there is more to my life, and if so, what is the more? You see, God created you and me to be upfront and personal with him. God in his love will enlighten your mind, incline your will, and influence your soul to come out of the darkness and into the light. God will draw your spirit to himself, as you were made to live in the light with him.

MY STORY

In college, I didn't know the Bible. I knew some stories and had gone to Sunday school as a child, but I didn't really know God. I wasn't necessarily looking for him either. I was looking for my truth to validate my existence, not his truth. I grew up in the age of enlightenment in the 70s and 80s, and it only seemed natural to want to become enlightened by truth. I do admit that I am a deep thinker with a philosophical bent. Maybe because the culture around me was in part devoted to the study of knowledge, reality, and existence. I had no idea that this desire for truth would take me on a journey that would lead me back to the way to God. My journey back to my Christian faith would take a decade and would take me through some trends and fads along the way. I rejected God for humanism.

My pursuit for spirituality began at the beginning of college when one of my mother's friends noticed my longing for spirituality. She wrote me a letter and gave me the book *The Prophet* by Kahil Gibran. She told me this book would answer many questions I had about life, love, death, and religion because it had helped her so much. I opened my heart to the teachings of this book, as I poured myself into it looking to have my longings fulfilled. This book was very spiritual, because it embraced the best of Christianity, Judaism, and Muslim teachings, but it left me confused with more questions than I had started with, and I put the book and my questions aside.

While in college my focus turned to psychology and philosophy because I had a deep love for people and the depths of the soul and the spirit. My spiritual longings may have gone underground for a time, as my pursuit was now for truth. I was exposed to some of the philosophers' writings, such as Jean-Paul Sartre's descriptions of life as a useless passion, which also left me unsatisfied and with a deeper passion for life and God.

The more I dug into philosophy, the emptier I would feel. I still wasn't sure what I was looking for. Like those around me, I relied on humanism and my own heart for truth. I also looked to the professors and the adults in my life who I believed had an edge on understanding and the knowledge of truth around me, while avoiding the Bible and the truth I was raised on. I needed an anchor point, an absolute truth, which was what my culture was fighting against. I seemed to always know deep down that God was beckoning me to draw near, I just hadn't found the path to him. Then while in college I had an opportunity for me to become "enlightened."

During my senior year in college, I found myself sitting in a room where everyone paid $250.00 to become spiritually enlightened. Erhard Seminars Training (EST) took place from late 1971 to late 1984 and was a four-day, 60-hour personal development course. It became popular in Hollywood and was now reaching college campuses. Hours and hours were spent teaching us to be ourselves and not play the role of past expectations, so that we could live whole and complete in the present. My psychology professors were running their own EST seminars, and as students, we were encouraged to participate.

What a perfect way to have my own spiritual awakening, I thought. I truly believed at the time that this would provide the spiritual insight I was looking for. The conferences became the training grounds to learn about letting go of our egos, our worthless human reasonings, and embrace "true spiritual awakening." They taught us that the beliefs that we held about our own lives and ourselves were rooted in ridiculous notions about reason, logic, and understanding.

I was intrigued at the variety of ages and the diversity of the group of people attending this weekend EST seminar. They all seemed to come for some kind of spiritual awakening. There were businessmen in shirt and ties and a tattooed motorcycle rider who sat next to me. All of us were looking for God outside of his written Word. Back then, only the rebels had tattoos, so the contrast between the businessman and the biker was intriguing. It just highlighted to me that all of humanity wants to know God. I must have looked like a naïve young girl, although I honestly felt like an adult for the first time in my life, because I was taking an active role in my spiritual growth.

The goal behind this EST experience was that at the end of the training where we were having our logic torn apart, we would be left with the "secret," which was that we are responsible for our life outcomes. That you simply had to "get it" and that was the secret. This process took all weekend to empty our minds and used many techniques, like sensory deprivation, to remove anything that would simulate our senses. We would lie on the floor in the dark with no sound except the meditations of the trainer. Yes, this was (and is) a type of brainwashing to clear away anything that we had thought to be true, so that we could define our own truth (or reality). In doing so, we were supposed to find our spiritual enlightenment. They said our enlightenment was this: "The truth is that there is no truth, and we are all a part of the divine." I couldn't reach the goal of EST because it didn't satisfy my inner longing to know truth and to know the will of God for my life, which meant getting to know God.

Many in the room smiled and said, "I get it," as they chose to agree with this new truth and settle into the void of emptiness. "I don't get it," said one of the participants at the end of a long day of emptying our minds and decoding our thought processes. The response was "Good. There's nothing to get, so you got it."

I didn't get it. I was left confused and angry at myself for spending the money and time to be left with nothing as the goal. I was mad at them for believing that God was nothing, and I was also mad at myself for spending my entire weekend lying on the floor trying to meditate on nothing. Emptying my mind somehow did not give me the feeling of bliss and elation that was promised. I felt no connection to anything that happened that weekend and left feeling completely void of any meaning. I had entered their secret, I didn't find God there, and I knew that I was not godlike.

I didn't know that God never told us to empty our minds. God told Jacob, one of the spiritual fathers in the Bible: "I never told you (Jacob) to 'Seek me in emptiness, in dark nothingness.' I am God. I work out in the open, saying what's right, setting things right."[10] God is not secretive, and there is no secret. God doesn't want us to empty our minds. Void and emptiness are not part of God's plan. Here is why: First, we see his intent in creation. The universe was void and empty, and God brought order, balance, and purpose. God took a desolate barren void of emptiness and brought order and balance through creation, the book of Genesis, and our present Earth testifies. It goes against our nature to go back to nothingness.

We can see that God had a plan to fill the earth and fill us, not empty it. We can expect the earth to turn and the sun to rise every day. If we want to live life to the fullest, we need to be filled with the fullness of God. God says that he has not spoken in secret. He has spoken, and out of his mouth came the foundations of the earth. He has created you so that you can have a placed to fill the earth with life, creativity, and bring balance. We are to fill our minds, not empty them or try to go back to a place that is without form and empty. God didn't go to all the trouble to create and make you and me just to leave us empty. He made us to be with him and know his will.

God loves us so much that he has provided us a way to fill our minds so that we can be content whatever the circumstances. He tells us it is best to fill our minds on things true, noble, reputable, authentic, compelling, gracious—the best, not the worst; the beautiful, not the ugly; things to praise, not things to curse. Put into practice what you learned from me, what you heard and saw and realized. Do that, and God, who makes everything work together, will work you into his most excellent harmonies.[11]

Looking back, it was as if God was keeping me for himself. I never did buy into this truth, and even writing this statement warms my heart, because I recognize that God was always right there with me drawing me away from darkness and into the light of his truth. There was a way that God had made available to me. It would take a few more years for me to find out for myself.

I didn't know it at the time, but God wasn't just looking for me to surrender my ego; he was looking for a divine exchange where I would give him my life and receive his sacrifice for mine. This meant sacrificing my truth and my thoughts about God and exchanging them for his. I didn't have to empty my mind but rather to begin to fill it with what he has to say about life, relationships, and me. I liken this to a glass of dirty water and the concept of displacement. I didn't have to empty the glass before I could get pure water; I could simply pour pure water into the glass and the filling up of what is pure and clean would displace what was toxic. God was not looking for me to empty myself but for me to be filled with the fullness of him.

Laying down our truth is most likely the hardest part of our spiritual journeys. Our pride has a way of rising up. We want to stand up for ourselves and want our own truth. It's easier and doesn't require us challenging the way we have been living. I doubted. I needed to know if giving up my truth was worth having his. It is okay to give yourself permission to doubt God, but I don't want you to stay there. Let's dig together because we know that there is truth out there about him.

MY JESUS ENCOUNTER

I wasn't seeking Jesus the Truth. I had not made Jesus my God. Jesus stepped into my heart one day unannounced. I had just entered a new season in my life. I was newly married and had my first child. We had bought our first house, and it seemed liked I had everything I dreamed of attaining. The man I love, the child I longed for, a new home and the resources to be home with my child and become the mother I always wanted to be. It was only a month into my new dream life that I started to recognize this void was still there from my days trying to become spiritually enlightened. My seemingly perfect husband worked nights, and I would spend evenings alone.

I thought the life that we had built would bring me satisfaction, but it didn't feel like what I had thought it would. Becoming an adult, a wife, and a mother wasn't enough to define me. I needed to find my real identity. I would spend the evenings alone where I would sit alone and channel-surf the television, because there was no internet to surf. Smartphones and social media were not available to entertain me and give me a form of connection to the outside world. I was alone, and that was exactly what I needed to have a spiritual encounter with the living God.

Each night I would come across a television program out of Santa Monica, California, that seemed to have some sort of spiritual empowerment. It was filled with life and powerful words of truth. It was called "Ever Increasing Faith." The pastor was a dynamic spirit-filled man named Dr. Fredrick K. C. Price who would talk about how we could have an abundant life supplied by faith in Jesus. There was something about the words he spoke that went straight to my heart. They were words out of the Bible that had life and substance on them. Something in me believed what he was saying. I learned things like happy and fulfilled are those who God has forgiven and who have confessed their separation from God. I started to sense my own brokenness, and I longed to be made whole before God.

I had once loved the drama of life. I found satisfaction watching soap operas in college because that was the only place to find drama to prove to myself that my life was normal and good. I kept all of my true feelings of insecurity and loneliness inside; my dishonesty devastated my inner life, causing me to be filled with frustration, anguish, and sometimes anger. Once I refused to hide, I openly acknowledged to this television pastor, "I believe in this Jesus." I had always wanted to do the right thing, but I didn't know that the right thing starts with finding our rightful place in the heart of God.

God will go to the ends of the earth to give us identity and truth, or to the other side of the coast through a television program to bring me his truth. I had this longing for the truth about God, and when I heard the words of the Bible, I just "knew" this was the truth. The Holy Spirit has a way of taking the Word of God and illuminating truth in a way that makes everything clear. Each night, Dr. Price would end the show with an invitation to receive Jesus as the Lord and Savior of our lives. He would always end with "We walk by faith and not by sight!" In 1987, I began my faith journey by inviting Jesus into my heart. God showed up to me in a real and tangible way. All I needed was someone who spoke his language and could show me the way to God. I had found my identity back to God.

LIVING IN THE LIGHT

This entire book has one purpose: to help you grow from a place of identity to a place of destiny. I said that destiny is not a location, as much as it is the unfolding of the will of God over your life lived in partnership and communication with God. God wants us to follow him into his love and into the light, into the only place where destiny can be found. Your destiny is found in the heart of God, and his love is waiting for you to discover that God is calling you out of darkness into his marvelous light.

This is not a feeling that we need to have; this is a choice. The choice of which light we will live in. My hope is that you will choose to live in is the light of being chosen, loved, and destined by God. We saw that our identities, names, gifts, and talents have led directly to our destinies; *you are chosen by God, and he wants you to choose him!*

DEFINING GOD

God chose you and all of humanity to love. God is described as Spirit, Light, Love, and many other ways. The Bible does not attempt to prove that God exists. Rather, it does describe his character, his nature, and reveals himself to humankind through his Son. It is through divine revelation that we are brought out of darkness into the light. God identifies himself as *"I Am Who I Am."*[12] I have always been, and I will always be, is how God describes himself. When Jesus came into the world, he bore witness to "I Am" and to what God wanted (and wants) to do. Jesus describes himself by adopting the phrase "I Am" and fills in the gap seven different ways. He uses the same verb "to be" and wants to be all of these for you.

- **"I am the bread of life."** As bread sustains physical life, so Christ offers and sustains spiritual life.

- **"I am the light of the world."** To a world lost in darkness, Christ offers himself as a guide.

- **"I am the door of the sheep."** Jesus protects his followers as shepherds protect their flocks from predators.

- **"I am the resurrection and the life."** Death is not the final word for those in Christ.

- **"I am the good shepherd."** Jesus is committed to caring and watching over those who are his.

- **"I am the way, the truth, and the life."** Jesus is the source of all truth and knowledge about God.

- **"I am the true vine."** By attaching ourselves to Christ, we enable his life to flow in and through us. Then, we cannot help but bear fruit that will honor the Father.[13]

The whole point is that God wants you to know him as all of these wonderful aspects, so that you do not have to go through life alone or unprepared. You can know this God and become known by him.

YOUR STORY

You, too, have a story and your story has power. There is power in the story of your life, and God wants to take everything that has come against you and impart courage, strength, and power for you to be the person you were meant to be. God will give you wisdom and strength to live your life to the fullest when you seek him with all your heart. The world needs your wisdom, your testimony, and your life story. You are needed, and you can be powerful with God. Some of you may have been hurt by the words, actions, and behaviors of those who looked to represent God in your life. No matter what happened, it was never God's intent for you to be hurt and walk away from him.

If you are far away from God, I want to say to you as a spiritual mother, I am sorry for what was stolen from you. I am sorry for the lies that were spoken to you that caused you to live in a place of separation from God. There is nothing that God wouldn't do for you to bring you back to his love. I am sorry for all the hurt that was done to you. I am sorry for all that life has done to you that has caused you to mistrust God. Your heart can be healed. We learned in the Section Two "Life with Others" about the power of forgiveness. To the degree that you choose to forgive others and forgive God, God will cause you to forget the pain it has caused you. Every time you forgive, which may be many times until you experience full freedom, God is going to restore in your life more that was stolen. Time doesn't heal all wounds, only Jesus by his grace, mercy, and love does. Remember, when you forgive people, forgive God for letting you down, and forgive yourself, you begin your healing journey.

Your story is filled with hope for a bright future. There are blessings, callings, and inheritance in your life that are waiting to be received. God is going to bless you. Don't limit your heart toward God. God has given you gifts that are waiting to be opened. There are treasures left to be discovered. God is going to take the unopened gifts, talents, and relationships that have been left behind and show you them again. When you walk with God, he will show you all that is true, right, and lovely. Don't be obsessed with all the negativity and everything that is wrong with the church, with Christianity, your family, and with yourself.

Ask God to show you the blessings, callings, and inheritance that is on your life. You can't do it without forgiveness. It's time to let it go. Don't drink the poison of unforgiveness thinking it is going to hurt the other person; unforgiveness will only hurt you. It's time to take back what was stolen and let go of the past. God is going to do amazing things in your life journey. There is a grace that comes with forgiveness.

I can hear you asking, "Why do bad things happen to good people if God is so great?" I have often asked God that very question. It is the reason that Jesus came to bring spiritual healing to that which was lost, broken, and stolen. I have come to see that he takes everything and will use it for good. I once heard these words spoken: *If you want to know part of your destiny, look at the areas where the devil has picked on you and caused you great pain.*

It is from this place of darkness, emptiness, and void that God will give you life and his divine nature to not only rebuild your life but give you double for your trouble. Let me share with you a principle found in the Bible that shows how God restores. There was a time in the life of King David, who was known as a man after God's own heart, when the enemy came and raided his camp. The enemy burned it to the ground and took his family. It was a very dark day for King David. He inquired of the Lord on whether he should go after the raiders. "And the Lord told him, 'Yes, go after them. You will surely recover everything that was taken from you!'" [14] Notice the words recover everything. This means, it's time to recover **everything.**

You can take this promise as you own. All that the devil has stolen from you will also be restored: your destiny, your joy, your hope, your faith in God. God is going to make up for all that the enemy has stolen. So, "Why do bad things happen to good people?" may not be the best question to be asking. The better question is, "What is God going to do with all of the bad that has happened in my life?" God is the restorer, the redeemer, and the one who will rebuild your life. I believe the greater the attack, the greater God will use you in the future. The world needs the light of God, and God wants to empower you and your story to be that light.

Your story has just begun. If I could talk to you face-to-face right now, I would say to you that God's grace and love is surrounding you, and God wants you to build your life on him. No matter what has come against you, God can turn it around and use it for good. God is inviting you into his story. I want you to know I am so proud of you for not giving up on God. You wouldn't be still reading this book if you had. It may seem like you are just holding on, but that is okay. His grace and love have you.

MAKE IT REAL

If you are ready to open your heart to possibilities of a God-filled life, I offer you this prayer:

> *Father, I pray for those who are reading this testimony that they would align their faith with a heart connection to You. I pray that you, Holy Spirit, would answer the spiritual longings of their hearts and expose them to the love of God, where intimacy with him is safe and secure.*

(Pause a moment to posture your heart toward God).

> *I pray for those who aren't feeling anything right now, that they would take a few moments and exercise their faith and allow their hearts to take them to places their minds can't go. That they would believe without seeing or feeling if need be. That your eternal promise that you are near to all who seek him, and those who search for him with all their hearts are certain to find him.[15] I ask that you would come, Holy Spirit, and guide them into a heart experience with you that would go beyond the words on this page into a real encounter with your love. And that only through the lens of your perfect love that the sin issue would be seen. Not as some kind of judgment coming from an angry God, but as the barrier to your heart that you want to take down. I pray that their spirits come alive as they acknowledge missing the mark of your perfect love and experience a touch, a sense, a picture, or a word that you love them and want to give them life and your divine nature. In Jesus's name, amen.*

Chapter 7

MEETING WITH GOD AS A FRIEND

SETTING THE STAGE

Before people ever started meeting God in a church, there was a place called The Tent of Meeting where people could encounter God. This place was not a building, it was not an organization, it was a place of God's presence inside of his tabernacle. The tabernacle was a blueprint to show a special tribe of people, the Hebrews, the holiness of God and reveal the condition of humanity. We have, at times, defined holiness as rules and ways of performing right before God. We have been schooled in Old Testament thinking. The tabernacle thinking has put us in the mindset that God only meets us in a box, and the only place you can find God is in the church. We have reserved holiness to the priests and pastors and what happens inside a church with the sacraments and rituals that are performed. We have lost the thought that God wants to meet with us, and holiness can become a lifestyle of friendship with God. I am going to take you behind the veil and show you how to meet with God as a friend.

This chapter is going to talk about this place I call a *tent in the woods*. We will talk about how to get in the tent and how to live in this tent in the presence of God. I believe people long for an authentic encounter with God without becoming religious. If you are ready, I am going to do something really interesting here. I am going to take the biblical blueprint of God's tabernacle and make it a spiritual metaphor for you to access the spiritual realm where God is. I am going to tell you how to not just know about God but how to be a carrier of his light and presence.

Oftentimes, people will tell me that I am a bright light, that they like my spirit, or they see me as a spiritual person. What they don't know is that I have built a place to meet with God, and what they are getting is a glimpse of the presence of God on me. People notice the presence of God when you have spent time with him. You, too, can be a bright light and carry the presence of God. This is God's story about a tent where you can meet with God, encounter his presence, and talk to him as a friend.

THE STORY OF THE MEETING WITH GOD

I first learned about the idea of God as personal when I was in my twenties. For a very long time, I thought God was "out there" someplace in the universe, basically unknown and unseen. I had known God in church, but I didn't know his ways or my way to him. I remember learning about a place called the tabernacle, which was the dwelling place of God. I came to understand that just as we consist of three parts—the body, soul, and spirit—the tabernacle consists of three sections: the "outer court," the "inner court or the holy place," and the "holy of holies," which depicts our human bodies that are made up of our bodies, souls, and spirits.

My body is the outer court that can be seen by anyone and experienced in various ways depending on who is with me. My soul is like the inner court that is more personal and private. My spirit is my most sacred place reserved for God alone. As I began to study the symbolism of the tabernacle and the time that God spent on the specific details of the tabernacle, I began to see that God was very specific on how he created us for his presence, that there was a way to pass through the separation, or the veil, that separates us from the spiritual realm where God's presence is attainable.

We can demonstrate our "light" to the world in how we relate to God, ourselves, and others. It was in the heart of God to set up a "tent in the woods" to teach us how to enter his presence and become a light to the world. God would show us how to take responsibility and care for ourselves so that what was reserved for special holy people could now be accessible to you and me. I love how practical God can be. When we consider the laws that God set up, like the ones that had dietary restrictions, we can see that God cares about our bodies because God wants it healthy and strong enough to carry his presence. Today, we can personally have some dietary restrictions where there are some things we can't eat, while others can. Some things that your body can tolerate that mine doesn't. God isn't looking to restrict us by living by some law about food; he is looking to our individual bodies to make us whole and healthy.

We can have a shift in our mindsets when we look to the heart of God behind what we would think are restrictions. God cares that I exercise my body and keep it strong and operating well. The outer court is the place where we can deal with what holds us back from God's best. It requires strength and discipline to care for my body and to care for my spiritual life. God wants to deal with my inner world—my soul where my thoughts and emotions have been tainted by the world. This is the place of the inner court. Most importantly, God wants to make us whole by accessing our spirits and filling us with his Holy Spirit so that we are aware of God and his presence. It is in the holy of holies where God embraces us as his own, guides us into truth, directs our path, changes us from the inside out, and empowers us to be a true light to the world around us.

The role of the tabernacle can teach us truths that we can relate to as a way of showing our desire to know God, experience him, and come into his presence. The tabernacle is symbolic of the way to God through relationship. We saw that first with a Hebraic priest who would go into the holiest place of God's presence for the people and finally through his Son, Jesus, where the separation to the holiness of God was ripped in two and everyone could now have access to the presence of this all-empowering, all knowing, and holy God.

The truth is that God is holy, and he wants to be our friend. Friendship with God always comes through relationship. God came to Earth in human flesh, through a relationship that we could best understand, that is the relationship of a loving father to a son to enable us to relate to him in our own humanness. We can never separate our humanness from the spiritual. We are human, and God is spirit, and it was through God becoming man that we could best relate to God.

God who is also the Holy Spirit, makes it possible to walk with him on Earth today. This triune God is perfect love in three persons: the Father, the Son, and the Holy Spirit. This three-dimensional love is meant to "flow to us" through the love of a Father, "flow through us" by the power of the Holy Spirit, and "flow out of us" to become like his Son, the "light of the world" to the world around us. Here is the deal: Jesus is our holiness, and he wants to awaken us and transform our consciousness, our thinking, our actions, and our passions to love God, love others, and love ourselves. It impresses me to see that wholeness can come in threes because it appears to be what brings fullness, harmony, and completeness. We see God in three persons, we see our humanity in three parts, and we see that God most often spoke generationally when speaking about three patriarchs who were the fathers of God's people. Abraham, Isaac, and Jacob were spiritual fathers, and God even mentions that where two or three people are gathered and relating to God, there in that place God is in the midst of them.[1]

God often speaks through natural objects or facts that represent the spiritual. There is great meaning in the tabernacle for us in terms of symbolism. If we can take the time to look at the symbolism and the time that God spent on the specific details of the tabernacle, we can see that God was very specific on how it points to the mysteries of Christ and access for all people. The Church has always been thought of as the meeting place for God for religious people. If we look at the structure and furnishings of the tabernacle, we can see that everything has special meaning and holds hidden secrets into how we, too, can experience God's presence. These truths that have been obscure for centuries that could only be accessed by select priests can now be unlocked for us today.

TENT IN THE WOODS

Today you don't need a leader to meet with God for you. You need a way to encounter God for yourself. The word *tabernacle* means "the dwelling place of God" in ancient Hebrew. God is looking to "tabernacling with humanity," and he wants to meet with you. In order to do so, you have to learn how to build your own place to meet with God. God created the tabernacle as a place to meet with his people, and he showed us how to meet with him face-to-face. Because people in ancient times lived in tents, it was only right that they could find God living in a tent as well. God set up this "tent in the woods" as a way for humanity to enter into his holiness and teach us how to have relationship. It was never God's intent to keep his presence from us; he was waiting for the right moment to press his love and presence back into his original design where humanity and divinity were one in a place called Eden. He did that by removing the barrier of sin. In simple terms, God made everything perfect for us; we messed that up, and he came back around to fix that for us.

THE HOLINESS OF GOD

Until God was made flesh in the person of Jesus Christ, God's presence was experienced on Earth quite differently than it is today. God appeared in a cloud by day, a pillar of fire by night, in a burning bush, and in a "still small" voice. The most terrifying time was when God showed up in the thunder, lightning, smoke, and fire on a mountain with Moses, where God delivered the Ten Commandments. It was also on this mountain that Moses received the plans for the tabernacle. The people were so afraid of God's holiness that they refused to go up the mountain to meet with God, and instead they built their own altar made of a golden calf in hopes that they would have some sort of God with them. They wanted a less scary god that was more like the gods of the people around them. It was the fear of God's holiness that caused the people to want a leader in order to meet with God, and when they watched Moses enter the tabernacle, they knew that God would be in their midst.

God was a friend to Moses and made his ways known to him.[2] Moses actually got to know God. God wants to meet with you and me, but there is a cost to meeting with God up front and personal. It will require us to see ourselves as we really are and deal with our own "golden calves" that we have crafted as a way of having some form of God with us. We all have, at one time or another, perhaps "knocked on wood," saved a good-luck charm, or tried to leave God out and rely on ourselves or other spiritual guides. We can, however, move beyond luck and become strong and courageous and look to find the God that is with us.

God's law and rituals were never intended to be our way of life; they were, however, the way of the ancient people. The Hebrew people had settled in lands associated with pagan people worshipping pagan gods. These rituals were made up of sacrifices and forms of worship to their gods. It was more the desire of the Hebrew people to sacrifice to the true and living God and to confirm their devotion and love to him that a system called the tabernacle was set up.

Today, it is far more meaningful to God for us to sacrifice and change our own hearts and minds from the negative to the positive that God rewards. It is the daily process of refining that goes on in a spiritual person. This, I believe, is what the tabernacle can mean to you and me. If we replace a negative emotion or thought with a positive emotion or thought, this can be our sacrifice to God. It is when we give up our own negative thinking and acting that it honors God and brings honor and dignity to all humanity, including ourselves. I can honor and choose to love a person, even if I do not love what they are doing. This act of love is a sacrifice. Making sacrifices and changing our minds and learning to love our neighbors as ourselves is far more than burnt offering and sacrifices. This is a sacrifice that is holy to God.

This is the story of sacrifice and true love. The story is one of God's intent: to be with his people through relationship, intimacy, and closeness. And because we violated his love boundaries, God designed a way to fully, holy, and completely redeem us back to himself. Just as sin separated humanity from God, God in his holiness had to separate himself from humanity because of his holy and perfect love. This whole story is about love and relationship with God, and if we deviate from that, we end up with religion and ritual.

The tabernacle was never meant to keep us from God. Rather, it was a system of boundaries set up to show us the purity, power, and dignity of God. It protected us from what being in the presence of God's holiness would have done to us without Jesus. At the cross, God tore open the veil so all could come into his holy presence. Once again, God crossed over that divide to show us we don't need to work our way back because he has made relationship available to us.

In ancient times, there were requirements to get "backstage" where God was. We had to learn, once again, that God's perfect love was not something to mess with. This system that I am calling the *tent in the woods* is the way back to God. I ask that you look at this system and keep in mind that relationship and restoration is always God's intent. If we don't look through the lens of love, we will misinterpret God's holiness as anger and only see religion without relationship.

Let's look at this system through the eyes of love, as we discover God's desire to be up front and personal with us. Let's journey into the tent and learn how to build our own place to encounter God. Inside the tabernacle were seven furnishings, and they all meant something. They still could mean something for us today. Don't let the ancient words distract you; rather, let's look at the symbolism and apply that to our language. There is a place we can go to in our hearts and in our minds to find God. Let's walk through the furniture together, as a symbol of the way to God. The seven pieces of furniture inside the tabernacle are as follows:

- The place of surrender to God (*Altar of Burnt Offering*)

- The place of coming clean (*Laver*)

- The place to taste and see that God is good (*Table of Showbread*)

- The place of illumination (*Lampstand*)

- The place of worship that unlocks the beauty of God (*Altar of Incense*)

- The place where the presence of God resided (*ark of the covenant*)

- The place where we can receive the grace of God (*mercy seat*)

THE PLACE OF SURRENDER TO GOD

The first stop is the Altar of Sacrifice, also called the Brazen Altar. This is the place where we must sacrifice our own desires to reach God on our own. This is simply the place where we can sit down and be really honest with God. This is the place where we can give our lives to God. This includes our physical bodies, as they are important to God and contain the temporary dwelling place of our souls (inner court or holy place) and our spirits (holy of holies). Remember that God wants us to keep our bodies healthy to function at their best and be healthy and strong enough to carry his presence.

God wants our physical tabernacles to be as healthy and strong as possible. This is also the place that we must face ourselves as we really are. The good, the bad, and the ugly. We have a choice when creating a tabernacle for God. We have to admit we are not perfect, and we need God. If we really want to live for something more than ourselves, we must admit we don't have what it takes to make the world a better place on our own. We all have failed to live up to a perfect standard. This is the place where we surrender to God and admit we need to make our wrongs right and that God has the power to do so.

So, brothers and sisters, since God has shown us great mercy,
I beg you to offer your lives as a living sacrifice to Him.
Your offering must be only for God and pleasing to Him,
which is the spiritual way for you to worship. Do not be
shaped by this world; instead, be changed within by a new
way of thinking. Then you will be able to decide what God
wants for you; you will know what is good and pleasing to
Him and what is perfect.[3]

THE PLACE OF COMING CLEAN

Also in the outer court is a large brass bowl called the "laver" to hold purifying water, which represents the Holy Spirit who assists us in the cleansing process. Part of the cleansing process is displacing negative thoughts that come into our consciousness and replacing them with things like, "Whatever is true, noble, reputable, authentic, compelling, gracious—the best, not the worst; the beautiful, not the ugly; things to praise, not things to curse. Put into practice what you learned from me, what you heard and saw and realized. Do that, and God, who makes everything work together, will work you into His most excellent harmonies."[4] God has provided in his written Word the wisdom, knowledge, and understanding to displace everything that keeps us from him.

We all have a little cleaning up to do when it comes to how we think about God, ourselves, and others and how we act in the world around us. God wants us to understand the importance of purity, and it would require the washing away of anything unclean. I can't imagine what went through the minds and hearts of the priests and the people when they considered their humanity and imperfections. The materials that were used for the laver are symbolic, as well as the function it provided. It is interesting that the women provided some of the materials needed.

"They made the bronze basin and its bronze stand from the mirrors of the women who served at the entrance to the tent of meeting." [5] It would require us to look at ourselves in the mirror and come face-to-face with ourselves, before we could come face-to-face with the perfect love of God in all of his holiness. The point was that we needed to be cleaned before entering God's presence and that starts with looking at ourselves right where we are. Although this ritual required the continually cleaning of the priests who would go before God on our behalf, that was abolished at the coming of Jesus who would fulfill all of God's requirements.

We see that fulfilled in this wonderful illustration of Jesus: "The Son is the dazzling radiance of God's splendor, the exact expression of God's true nature—his mirror image! He holds the universe together and expands it by the mighty power of his spoken word. He accomplished for us the complete cleansing of sins, and then took his seat on the highest throne at the right hand of the majestic One.[6] Jesus has come to make you pure, authentic, and alive, so that when God looks at you, he sees the mirrored image of his Son living in you.

For us, the laver can become the place where we sacrifice our fears and pride and admit we do not have what it takes to become whole, that we have failed God and failed ourselves, and ultimately that we have missed the mark of God's perfect standard, which that is called sin. Once we come clean by being honest with God, we are invited to wash our hands free of the guilt, shame, and pressure to be perfect and walk in purity. To get rid of all the junk we've allowed to live inside of us, we need God's presence to shine his light on those things that no longer serve us. This is symbolic of receiving a new heart.

This is the hardest part of coming face-to-face with God, because we must lay down our need to fix ourselves. It can take years of suffering the consequences of our own choices and seeing the pain and suffering in the world to get us to the point of humbling ourselves before him, but it doesn't have to. Jesus was humble in heart and asks us to take his yoke of humility upon ourselves and learn from him, for in his gentleness and humility we will find rest for our souls.[7] God isn't looking for you to be perfect; he is looking for your humility and vulnerability. God is not looking to tear you down. He is looking to build you up. You must decide if God is for you or against you. I am here to tell you that God is for you, and he will bring wholeness to you if you are willing to come clean and be honest, vulnerable, and take a risk to put your faith in him. Let's move on to the "inner court" or the "holy place."

THE PLACE TO TASTE AND SEE THAT GOD IS GOOD

Inside the "inner court" was a table of the finest bread that represented a few different things, one being the bread that was eaten by the priests and also a symbol of gratitude to God for daily bread. Jesus spoke in the Lord's prayer the words "Give us this day our daily bread." The table of "showbread" also represents the bread that came down from heaven. This is the substance of Jesus who called himself the "Bread of Life."[8] Bread and living water are seen as the gift from God. Bread is a sign of substance, nourishment, sharing, and life.

How does this pertain to us? We are to desire spiritual food. We will always hunger for the bread of life, substance, and spiritual nourishment. Jesus says that he comes to fill us entirely with life, spiritual realities, and significance. Bread is symbolic of God's provision, compassion and consistent care, and his presence. We see this in the story of Jesus feeding the five thousand with five loaves of bread and two fish.[9] Jesus saw that a crowd had gathered. Many were sick and hungry, and he had compassion on them. Jesus, the Bread of Life, healed them, provided food for them, and stayed with them a while so that they could experience his presence. Jesus came to make them whole.

Our souls have always thirsted for the living God; it's part of the longings of our hearts, and God is inviting you to draw close to him, to experience his love and the goodness that surrounds him. God offers you the substance of life, provision, protection, direction, peace, forgiveness, wisdom, understanding, knowledge, and so much more. "Oh taste and see that the Lord is good: blessed is the man/woman who trusts in Him!"[10]

THE PLACE OF ILLUMINATION

Also, inside the inner court we will find a candlestick made of pure gold. This was not a candlestick like we would have thought. It was a lamp with an oil reservoir and a wick that drew olive oil to the top. It was trimmed daily, and the light never went out. Jesus said, "I am the light of the world. Whoever follows me will never walk in darkness but will have the light of life."[11] This true light that has come into the world enlightens every human being to become a light to the world. This lamp simply put in the spiritual sense is "turning on the light" of our understanding of God. We need the light of God's Spirit to help unfold the meaning of God's words, and this is the job of the Holy Spirit.

When God's Word enters the heart of a person, it gives light and understanding to them. This is done by the power of God's Spirit, not our own knowledge. It's no wonder that Satan who disguises himself as an angel of light will make people think they have found the light, by feeding them words that they want to hear and not always the truth. When in reality it is only the Spirit of God that can touch the heart, illuminate our minds, and open our eyes to see ourselves as we are and eventually to see God as he is. God is inviting you to consider this privilege and responsibility to become a "light of the world" and "let your light shine brightly before others, so that your commendable works will shine as light upon them, and then they will give their praise to your Father in Heaven."[12]

THE PLACE OF WORSHIP THAT UNLOCKS THE BEAUTY OF GOD

Immediately in front of the holy of holies, but still in the inner court or holy place sits the Altar of Incense. The "holy place" and "holy of holies" are separated by a thick veil. Next to the veil, but still in the holy place, this altar was for burning incense to become a pleasant aroma before the presence of God in the holy of holies. Think of this as prayer and worship. "May my prayer be set before you like incense and the lifting up of my hand as the evening sacrifice."[13] The burning of incense has always been considered a doorway to spirituality. It is often something that people do when meditating to heighten their senses to connect to the spiritual and as a means of experiencing peace, relaxation, or mindfulness. Let's say that this is the place of prayer, where you have a sense of communicating with God. When an individual really prays from the heart with faith, a change is experienced deep within their soul and can affect those they come in contact with. For instance, have you ever prayed with faith that everything would turn out okay, and suddenly you have this warm, calming presence that comes over you? Your prayers of faith in God touched his heart, and it is in this place that you can experience his presence.

Not only do your prayers touch the heart of God but so does worship. Worship is my heart expressing something to God, where I find unity with him personally. We worship God not because he needs it; it is because of what it will do for us. It will connect us to the love of God that heals, restores, and empowers us. Worship is not just a song from a written script that we sing to God and join in with others where we all sing the same song. It is a heart connection that connects to God. God always looks upon the heart. When we can uniquely express our hearts to God in a way that is like no other, this becomes true worship. It is not something that God demands or something where we all sing the same song in the same way; it is the expression of a unique heart that ushers in the reality of God. God longs for our worship, not because he needs it, but rather because we need it.

Worship unlocks the beauty and majesty of God because we connect with WHO HE IS. We don't worship just to "get." However, worship can be the place where healing happens, in the heart, soul, and spirit, because love is the healing agent. It is the place where discouragement can be lifted, hopelessness and weariness can be lifted out of your heart, and you can experience the peace and presence of God. God does miracles when we worship. God wants your worship to become a place of beauty, so that as you behold (gaze upon him), you will be able to express his beauty through your voice, words, actions, and creative expressions to the world around you and make the world a better place.

THE PLACE WHERE PRESENCE OF GOD RESIDED

Now we come to the holy of holies, the place where God would make his presence known. This last room held the ark of the covenant, which was a special chest that was covered in pure gold and had a lid called the "mercy seat." The ark had two golden angels on the lid with their wings outstretched covering the mercy seat. It was on the mercy seat that a high priest would place a (blood) sacrifice for the people once each year. The angels symbolized protection, where their wings were used to protect the mercy seat and the ark of the covenant. Inside the ark was placed the stones that held the Ten Commandments and several other items that held special significance for the Hebrew people.

In the days of the tabernacle, there was a separation of the holy place and the holy of holies in the form of a thick veil. This veil was hugely significant because "The moment that Jesus passionately cried out, took His last breath, and gave up His spirit (at the cross), at that moment the veil in the holy of holies was torn in two from the top to the bottom, the earth shook violently, rocks were violently split."[14] It was obvious that it was the hand of God that tore the veil from top to bottom offering a way for all to come into his presence. Now everyone has access to the presence of God. Truths that were hidden and obscure for centuries can be unlocked. For that which was at one time only for select priests can now be available to all. When Jesus died on the cross, that was the fulfillment of the tabernacle deeper truths of the holy of holies or entering the presence of God.

ATONEMENT FOR SIN

The words *blood sacrifice* has become a morbid term that conjures up all kinds of unpleasant thoughts, because it has been distorted and used by demonic cults as a counterfeit way to access spiritual power. It would do us good to not be ignorant of the power of the blood of Jesus. We must understand that God in his perfect love and justice would once and for all offer a final sacrifice, and there would be no more need for the blood of goats and lambs. In his perfect plan, God would sacrifice his own need for justice. If there was another way, I am sure that God would have provided that, but he chose to take on the suffering of all of humanity and destroy evil once and for all. If only we could grasp the power of this kind of love. It could not only be love that saved the world but would take God to become a man to take back what was given away by humanity.

God cannot condone wrongdoing, and his eyes are too pure to look upon any evil. God in his mercy made a way for us to see him in all of his splendor and glory and encounter pure love. This is the love that not only saved the world but will heal us and restore us back to beauty, the beauty of his creation, and back to the original DNA of being made in the image of God. If you are willing to receive these truths, you can receive a new heart and God will put his Spirit in you.[15] You have a way to encounter God for yourself. God is looking to "tabernacle with humanity." He wants to meet with you. In order to do so, you will need to build your own place to meet with God and look to the tabernacle as a way into the presence of God. Something happens when we get up close and personal with God. We find that we are loved and valued and have a purpose to fulfill, and that begins with coming into the light.

THE PLACE WHERE WE CAN RECEIVE THE GRACE OF GOD

Something happens when we can come into the presence of God. We find what was broken becoming healed, what was wrong becoming right. We all need the mercy of God, and we receive that when we come to Jesus who established a new covenant with his blood sprinkled upon the mercy seat, blood that continues to speak from heaven a better word: forgiveness. We all want the mercy of God when we are in the wrong, but we usually want justice for others when they have done wrong to us.

We live in this double standard where we want mercy for us and justice for others, that has caused such hatred and division that without the justice of God that poured out his own blood to provide the mercy for all humanity, we are left living in a double standard. It is not easy to forgive those who have wrongfully hurt or shown unkindness to us. Forgiveness of any kind is difficult, always humbling, and sometimes can feel degrading and humiliating. When forgiveness is given or asked, you can release the pain and allow the cleansing that brings joyous freedom. Looking at your own life you may have felt a sense of being crucified, stripped of dignity, and wondered where is God? God was in Christ Jesus reconciling you back to wholeness.

WHY DO YOU NEED THE MERCY OF GOD?

What is the definition of *mercy*? Mercy is the compassion of God that is ready to help us in our time of trouble, when we deserve just treatment for our wrongs. We must all understand that it was the justice of God that provided the way for mercy. Our world can become a better place when we receive this gift of mercy once and for all through the blood of Jesus. All kinds of things happen when God's mercy is present: creative gifts, passions to grow, love to find its home. Fear leaves and hope arises. God wants us to know that his mercy triumphs over all sin and judgment. We need God's mercy. None of us are perfect, and we are all in need of mercy. It is only through the final sacrifice of Jesus that we have access to God's mercy. The mercy seat of God can have a place in our lives in that we can call upon the Lord for mercy and help in our time of need. God is very willing, even delighted, to give us his help and mercy.

SUMMARY

The reality of the tabernacle is done away in the person of Jesus. Instead of praying in a building where God can live, God wants to come and dwell in us. God wants to replace the tabernacle with you and me, where together "this entire building is under construction and is continually growing under his supervision until it rises up completed as the holy temple of the Lord himself."[16] We were never meant to live in our own spiritual realities; we were created to live together, but it always starts with how we come to him on our own. The tabernacle can help us to unpack what it looks like to live in the presence of God, with the fullness of Jesus being one with us. And out of this oneness with Christ, we can live in the light.

The holy of holies is that inward part of us, our hearts and spirits where the Holy Spirit is looking to dwell. His truth, cleansing, and purpose are all very personal. God knows his purpose for each one that he has placed deep inside of us for a particular time and season. I invite you into the reality of God's spiritual realm and into the circle of love. I invite you to come up front and personal with God. The mystery of God is no longer a secret. God is not "out there" somewhere; he is no longer living in a *tent in the woods*. God is here with you always. The spiritual realm is very real. We tend to think of God as being up in heaven or somewhere out there in the universe. God's Word says the Kingdom of God (or the realm of God's ruling reign) is "at hand." This means that God is reachable and can be as close as you want.

You are living with God, whether you see him or not. You are not alone. You are never alone. God is with you right now. The truth is that now you know how to come to him. God loves you and has provided the way for you to be with him. You can't access what you aren't aware of. If you can see how the spiritual way of approaching God works, you can have the faith and power to encounter God. We are all created to live in the presence of God. God is forever pursuing you with his love and mercy. God's love is always working in your life by his Spirit to draw you out of the darkness and into his glorious light. It's time to live for his greater purpose; put down your tent pegs, and erect your own tent with God.

YOUR PRAYER TO GOD

Here is a simple prayer If you want to step closer to God and investigate this ancient path:

God, I want to know you as you are. If you are real, make yourself known to me. Amen.

If you want to walk with God:

God, I believe that Jesus is who he says he is and did what you say he did. I want to walk with you, God, so I admit that without you I am broken, and with you I can be made new. I give you all my confusion and ask that you give me a new heart of love, purpose. and truth. Amen.

If you are already a believer in Christ and want an encounter with God:

Father, I admit I have walked away from you, and today I choose to come back to you. I need your power in my life and to know you more. Fill me afresh with your Holy Spirit. I give you full access to every area of my life in exchange for your empowerment. Show me how to live in the truth, live in your love, and live to make you known. Amen.

If you prayed this prayer, this is the moment of your divine exchange. This is where the veil that separated you from God came tearing down, and you now have free access into his presence. If you were not ready to pray the prayer, just know that the love of God is pushing against the veil waiting for you to come back into the love relationship that started from the beginning of all time.

If you surrendered your way for his, then his Spirit became united with yours. Receive the fullness of life who is Jesus. I trust you feel his overwhelming peace or a sense of calm. I believe that in the days following you will be changed. This feeling right now will slowly begin to fade away, so it is important that you find a tribe who also want to live in his presence and live in his love. Once you find his presence, you will see that this is the gift of love that we not only receive but is a gift we have to give away to others. This is the true light.

Chapter 8

HEARING THE VOICE OF GOD

"I want to talk to God, but it's been so long."
– Kanye West, "Jesus Walks"

When we talk to God it is called prayer. When we listen, God speaks, and over time it becomes a relationship. I spent years talking to God and praying for many things, like for God to help me get through a difficult time. I spent time praying to God to help me be brave and begged God to heal a loved one who was dying. It was almost like I had reserved prayer for the really serious times like when I had nothing else to say when someone gives us bad news.

How many times have you heard it said, "I will pray for you" or "My prayers are with you"? I wonder if people really do pray, and if they do, what are the results? It never dawned on me that I could stop to listen to see if God was speaking to me. What if I told you that God wants to speak to you, and you can learn to hear his voice? Hearing from God doesn't have to be super spiritual. We can hear him in the everyday simple things. God wants to be involved in everything we are involved in. The problem is most likely we have not been intentional about talking and listening to God. It is much easier to look for signs that God hears us, than to look to see if God is speaking. Can we have communication with the God of the universe? The answer is yes. There is a voice that speaks truth, calls us higher, and is always filled with love. It is the voice we want to hear most because it is the voice of love, and it is the voice we were born to hear.

DOES GOD REALLY SPEAK TO ME?

Our faith will never be exciting to us until we learn how to have a close two-way communication with God. We usually don't think about talking with God, until we need something. Life's difficulties can find us needing to breathe and needing to know that we are not alone. There are times we need guidance and direction, and sometimes we just need to know that God is there for us. The truth is that it's always easier to hear from God through other people, but to hear God will take us learning how to hear from God for ourselves.

We are all born with the ability to see, hear, feel, and perceive God's revelation through our senses. It is part of our God-given design. The key to hearing the voice of God is that you are pursuing a relationship with him. Those who are in Christ will hear his voice, and many times it comes through one of our senses. Jesus says it this way: "My sheep hear my voice, and I know them and they follow me."[1] I believe that we can all hear God in many different ways through our senses, see him in nature, and hear him through other people, as well as learning to hear him in the still small voice. If we want to access the wisdom, knowledge, and understanding behind what we hear, we must position ourselves to look to where God is and to see what he wants to show us.

Jesus is the way to God, so fixing our eyes on him will clear the spiritual airways of all the static. I liken this to having our spiritual antenna positioned above the heavens into the place where God is.

We are living in a time when we must learn how to take responsibility for what we are listening to. There are so many voices out there, and it is hard to know which one is true; that is why we need to access the wisdom of God that comes through Jesus who is the truth. I remember when my son graduated from high school, I wrote in his graduation card a key Scripture verse for his future. "Trust in the Lord with all your heart, and don't lean (solely) on your own understanding. In all your ways acknowledge Him, and He will make your paths straight."[2] Leaning into God and seeking his wisdom, understanding, and knowledge will lead you in every decision you make. This leaning into God will require us to learn how to receive God's intelligence. I continue to refer to this verse and remind all of my children, both natural and spiritual, that we need to lean into God and learn to hear his voice. Hearing from God is a game changer. Some can think they are not worthy to hear the voice of God for themselves, but if you are seeking him, you will find the way to his voice.

The problem for most of us is all the clutter that fills our minds. It is more than simply trying to eliminate the internal noise. We must fill our minds with the way that God thinks, so that we can recognize the voice of God when he speaks. We need a foundation for which we can receive revelation and judge what we are hearing as truth and that foundation is his Word. God will never go against his nature, his character, and his Word. So, if we turn from our negative thinking and start to think more like God, his voice will have a place to land. God tells us to renew our minds. He says it this way: "Do not be shaped by this world; instead, be changed within by a new way of thinking. Then you will be able to decide what God wants for you; you will know what is good and pleasing to Him and what is perfect."[3]

I have found that when God speaks to me it almost always comes first through the filter of his love for me. The first time I was intentional to sit down and listen, all that kept bubbling up in my heart were the words "I have loved you from the beginning and will love you always." I was actually embarrassed to hear those words and would push them away and tell myself I can't hear from God; I am only telling myself what I want to hear. It felt very awkward to me because I had no idea that God speaks through the language of love. God has an ocean of love to share with you, and his voice almost always comes first to tell us how much he loves us, so that you will be able to say *this must be God*. God wants to speak to you and show you his perfect love.

God wants to be upfront and personal and share his will for your life with you. Most people have settled for secondhand revelation. They have relied on their own opinions or the guidance and direction of others. Some rely on their hearts to guide them, hoping that the result will "feel" good to them. This can lead us down a bumpy road of self-promotion, unrealistic goals and expectations, and you can end up in a pothole of great heart ache, but God can make a straight path before you and give you the wisdom you need. I am not saying that our own opinions don't matter. What I am saying is that what feels good is not always the wisdom of God. God has true wisdom for you, because he is the one who is wisdom. God has prepared some things for you, and he will keep them ready for you when you come to him. However, as it is written: "What no eye has seen. What no ear has heard, and what no human mind has conceived the things God has prepared for those who love Him."[4] God has some things that he wants to reveal to you.

We all need truth for ourselves, and we can receive present revelation where God can make known to us what is best by sitting and learning to discover God's voice for ourselves. God says, call to him and he will answer you and tell you great and unsearchable things you do not know.[5] God wants to be your voice of reason, your voice of truth, and your voice of love and acceptance. I believe that there is a generation who has grown bored simply relying on the revelation of others. We must find out who God is for ourselves. We can do that by taking time aside and moving past praying into listening for him. When we know we have heard him for ourselves, the words touch everything in us and makes God personal. Are you ready to place your ear next to his, and hear his voice?

ARE YOU READY TO OWN WHO GOD CAN BE FOR YOU?

Many people think that when God speaks to us it comes in a download from some external force. When God speaks it doesn't come from the outside, as you may have come to believe. God doesn't speak to us in English words that come to us in a conversation. When God speaks you already have words, images, and thoughts imprinted in your psyche. When I say *dog*, you can actually experience a dog without the dog being present because it has been imprinted in your soul: your imagination, memory, and reasoning. We can all experience a different dog depending on what is imprinted individually.

When God wants to speak to us, he is going to use the language of his Son, which is all wisdom, understanding, and knowledge. We are told in Proverbs, "For the Lord gives wisdom, from his mouth come knowledge and understanding."[6] Jesus is wisdom, and the way we know it is God is that we can find the interpretation for what we are receiving in the life and character of Jesus. When God talks to you, it will be processed through your own psyche. The reason we miss God speaking is because God sounds a lot more like one of us. We see in the Bible the first time that God speaks to Samuel, a young boy who is being raised by a man names Eli. One night while Samuel was lying down, he heard the Lord call to him, "Samuel." The boy got up and went to Eli three times saying, "Here I am, you called me." Because God had not been revealed to Samuel yet, God sounded like Eli because he was the only reference point of authority that he had in his life. It was Eli who realized it was God calling the boy, so he told the boy to go lie down, and if he calls him again, say "Speak Lord, for your servant is listening."[7]

I believe that God wants to speak to you and make you a voice for your generation—a voice of truth, a voice of hope, and a voice of encouragement. If you are looking to hear the voice of God, you must get to know how God became fully human to teach us how to become part of his divine nature. His language will always be found in the wisdom of his Son. If you are looking to find your voice, we must deal with some of those challenging voices of negative self-talk, criticism, and condemning words that can come from our own negative thinking. They can also come from words spoken over us, or even words from the voice of the devil himself. These voices can swirl around in our heads and cause us to spiral downward into a state of inadequacy and self-deprivation. We can learn to silence these voices by learning the voice of truth. Let's look at how God speaks to us, so that when we encounter the truth, we will recognize a lie. This voice comes with love and wisdom, a voice that brings clarity and healing and many times is in the still small voice. This is the voice of God.

THE STILL SMALL VOICE

We can find God speaking in a specific way to a man named Elijah in the Bible. God had told Elijah to go and stand on a mountain in the presence of the Lord, as he was going to pass by. I remember going to Israel, to the wilderness, and standing on a mountain in deep silence. The mountains in the wilderness look like the desert. All you see is dust for miles and miles and all you hear is silence. We were asked by the tour guide to silence our hearts and listen for God. I remember hearing the loudness of silence in the vastness of the desert, as I sensed that God was there in the silence. In that silence, I realized that God was much bigger than I could ever imagine. God brought revelation in a *still small voice* when I was on that mountain waiting to hear from God. That revelation was that God is always with me, and he is powerful in his silence. He is infinitely bigger than the vastness of mountain range after mountain range that I experienced that seemed to go on to eternity.

Elijah also experienced God on a mountain. He was in a really hard place and had felt alone and depressed after he challenged the gods of the culture, in which he was living. Elijah was being chased by his enemies, and it was then that God was about to reveal himself to Elijah as he stood on his mountain. Elijah needed a personal encounter with God. It was there that a great and strong wind tore into the mountain and the Lord was not in the wind, and after the wind and earthquake, the Lord was not in the earthquake.

After the earthquake came a fire, but the Lord was not in the fire. After the fire there came a *still small voice*, and suddenly he heard the Lord say, "What are you doing here, Elijah?"[8] What conquered the heart of Elijah was not the wind, the earthquake, or the fire that he had experienced when he challenged the gods of the culture. It was the still small voice that won his heart back to God. God was in the *still small voice*, a whisper if you will. We don't need a dramatic demonstration or revelation to know that God is speaking to us. Sometimes it comes through a quiet inner thought that we recognize we didn't have before and wins us back to God and to his extraordinary love.

GOD'S VOICE COMES IN A SPONTANEOUS FLOW

Mark and Patti Virkler developed a four-key method to hearing the voice of God. This is a great process for learning to hear the voice of God through journaling. The first key to hearing God's voice is to go to a quiet place and still our own thoughts and emotions. The second key to hearing God's voice is as you pray, fix the eyes of your heart upon Jesus, seeing in the Spirit the dreams and visions of Almighty God. The third key to hearing God's voice is recognizing that God's voice in your heart often sounds like a flow of spontaneous thoughts. And the fourth key, two-way journaling or the writing out of your prayers and God's answers, brings great freedom in hearing God's voice.[9]

God has given us eyes in our hearts to see into the spiritual realm. There is an active spirit world around us that is full of angels, demons, the Holy Spirit, the omnipresent Father, and his ever-living Son, Jesus. When we access the omnipresent Father through his Son, Jesus, we can access true revelation. "For your heart will always pursue what you value as your treasure. The eyes of our spirit allow revelation-light to enter into your being. If your heart is unclouded, the light floods in."[10] When we pursue the voice of God, we can receive revelation that comes to turn the light on in our hearts, which illuminates our minds. He places in our hearts his thoughts, and then our minds become the vehicles that interprets the meditations of God's heart towards us. As our minds become filled with what's in our hearts, we can learn to recognize our thoughts and tendencies as coming from God, only as we allow them to flow with what we believe about God. That is why it is so important to get an accurate view of God. God's voice will always build us up, even if it means a course correction.

Let me give you a personal example of how God's voice comes through a spontaneous flow. When I was first learning to hear the voice of God,

I was in a class with others. Our instructor asked us to find a place of rest that works for us. The first, and hardest, lesson was to be still enough to quiet my internal noise. Learning to quiet our minds and emotions is a process. If your mind is running, it can help to write down what is running through your mind, so that you can address it later. When a thought comes of what you need to be doing, you can keep a pad of paper next to you, and as those thoughts come to mind, quickly jot them down on a piece of paper and then go back to quieting your internal world. This first process is all about learning to cultivate an attitude of inner stillness. This is where the spontaneous flow of God's thoughts come to us.

I then present my heart to God and ask him to speak to me, and I activate my faith, which is my believing that he will speak to me. If I don't hear anything or nothing is bubbling up, I keep an open mind and heart and expect him to speak at some point. This is where faith comes in. I start with a journal and a pen and ask God, "What are your thoughts for me right now?" Remember that the voice of God comes through the language of love. Just as I had felt the awkwardness of God's words of love toward me, you, too, may find that in that awkward silence the thoughts that bubble up in your heart are words like "I love you, my beautiful one."

I challenge you to not allow those words to be intercepted by your mind with thoughts like "This isn't God. These are just my own thoughts." It wasn't until I was encouraged to just go with what was bubbling up in my heart and write from the spontaneous flow that I began to understand that God speaks to the condition of our hearts first. This is to tell us how much he loves us. The voice of God is always love, even when it comes to correct and redirect us. You can trust that God is speaking to you. He will make sure that you are not confused or deceived.

WHEN GOD TALKS TO US

We need to understand how God speaks to us. When God talks to us. He talks to us through our hearts (spirits), and our minds interpret his thoughts. How do we know that what we are hearing are not our own voices? The very first thing is that what we are hearing has to line up with God's character and his nature. There are many times his voice will be that of kindness and loving. Second, we have to believe that we can hear from God. We all go through wondering if it's God or us. If we have doubt that it's God, the enemy will play with our minds, and we will think we don't hear from God. Many times, when God speaks to us it *sounds like our own voices*. It is a process, and that process looks like *believing* that we heard from God.

God can speak in many ways including through our senses:

- Circumstances
- Desires
- Dreams
- Still small voice
- Discernment
- Scripture
- Seeing
- Hearing
- Feeling
- Perceiving

God speaks to our hearts (which are our spirits), and many times, God will speak to the *desires* inside of us that have been placed there by him.

A DESIRE FULFILLED

We can't expect that God will always answer us in words. Many times, it is a discerning we have, a sense or a feeling that this is God. God will sometimes speak to our desires with a knowing that we can have them. It is like our "knower" knows it is God speaking to us. For example, when I was having children, I was blessed with two sons. My husband, being a very practical man, thought we were done having children. He thought a family of four was perfect, and yet I had this longing in my heart that we were not done having children. I talked to God about changing my husband's heart, and I had peace that this was God's will.

I waited a year, then another year, and the longer I waited in the natural it seemed like the peace of God was no longer as clear to me. But the desire never left, and although I didn't get a yes from God, I did have the sense that one day my husband was going to change his mind. I "felt" that God had heard me, and one year later, my daughter was born. God not only changed my husband's mind but increased his love for his children by adding the joy of a little girl! Sometimes God speaks to us through senses that touch our hearts and we know that it is God. We can feel his peace that brings about an assurance that he has heard our heart's desire and is answering our prayer.

SOMETIMES GOD'S VOICE COMES THROUGH OUR SENSES

Many times, we will seek God for direction when it comes to decision-making. Have you ever had a decision to make about a new job, a move, or starting or ending a relationship? God wants to assist us in the path that he has for us. However, the hardest part can be in discovering what that path looks like; it will take trust. Remember the proverb of wisdom I gave my son at graduation? This Proverb says, "Trust in the Lord with all your heart, and lean not on your own understanding; in all your ways acknowledge Him, and He shall direct your paths."[11]

One of the ways that God directs us is through the presence of peace. We can experience God through our senses like the presence of peace. If we have peace in our hearts about a decision, we can move forward with it, and if in the process we find we no longer have peace, we can simply push the "pause button" and wait and let our emotions settle. Asking for counsel from a trusted advisor will help in the process. It is important to not make a decision in the heat of our emotions. A time out will determine if it is our emotions or our nerves that have gotten the best of us. Wise counsel will help to determine if we are simply struggling with our lack of courage or God is saying "stay" where you are. Peace is usually the evidence that it is God, as he is described as the "Prince of Peace," and his presence can direct us through our senses.[12]

More often than not, it is our heart condition that God speaks to. Why the heart? Throughout the Bible, it is primarily the heart condition that God addresses, for it is the heart that trusts God. "We believe with our hearts, and so we are made right with God. And we declare with our mouths that we believe, and so we are saved."[13] It is the heart that God longs to heal. There can be brokenness in our hearts, like anxiety, sadness, anger, and fear. God can use natural means to bring about supernatural healing. God wants to heal our hearts. He can begin that process through the process of receiving the love of God, and that can come from places we least expect. God wants us to believe in him and believe that he has good things for us, so that we can bring his goodness to others. He speaks to us through our hearts in many different ways.

Examples of evidence when God speaks to the heart:

- Certain songs that bring us to tears
- Being awestruck by the beauty of nature
- Crying at a sad movie
- Concern
- Burden for something
- Joy
- Grief
- Times of intuition: a feeling of dread, or a feeling that something is about to happen before it does
- Unexplainable fear
- Undeniable love

God wants to bring you to a place where you are not shaken by things of this world, or shaken by anxiety, fear, loveless people, and confusion. God longs for you to hear his voice, and he wants you to find your own voice. He has provided the means to find your place in the world by hearing what he has to say about you. His voice of love will heal your heart and build you up to have the courage to walk in wisdom, understanding, and knowledge and walk into your destiny. Let's look at the different voices we hear.

THREE VOICES

We must understand that there are three possible "voices" we may hear:

- Our voice
- Satan's voice
- God's voice

Our voice will have certain characteristics. Our voice comes through the processing of information based on the knowledge you already have. It will most likely be rational, logical, willful, problem solving, analyzing, and even thoughtful. It will come with our own intentions, which could be good, bad, or neutral in its intentions but have our own self-interest as the motivating factor.

Satan's voice often "pops" into your mind uninvited, sometimes disrupting a positive thought and bringing confusion to a constructive thought. This unwanted voice comes with thoughts you do not want to entertain. They are negative, vengeful, fearful, lustful, anxiety producing, critical, condemning, pushy, hateful, accusative, compulsive, and bring confusion. This voice will push you, rush you, frighten you, confuse you, condemn and discourage you. All are contrary to the nature of God and his Word.

God's voice will still you. It is loving, peaceful, joyful, uplifting, strengthening, encouraging, comforting, creative, and full of wisdom, revelation, and enlightenment. It is always consistent with his nature and his Word. God's voice will reassure you and at times convict you of the wrong you are doing. Even when discipline is needed, it always comes through the voice of love. God's voice always looks to edify, encourage, and bring us comfort.

STUMBLING BLOCKS TO HEARING GOD'S VOICE

A stumbling block to having the faith to hear God's voice, is our concern with our past mistakes. God's voice may show us our past and the wrong we have done, not to punish us, but rather to heal us and to get us to make things right. His voice always comes with a solution that can provide knowledge, understanding, and is always full of his wisdom. God's voice looks to propel us into the glorious future he has reserved for us.

We can think that we can't hear from God, simply because we don't hear the way other's do. God is always speaking, and sometimes we have to let go of the ways we think he speaks. If you love the outdoors, you may see God speaking to you through nature. If you have a love for the arts, you can see more than the beauty of the art, but it can speak to you a message of hope, healing, and encouragement. God always speaks to who you are. He always speaks to you in your own language.

What do we do about Satan's voice? "We are to resist it. So then, surrender to God. Stand up to the devil and resist him, and he will turn and run away from you."[14] You come against the source of the negative thought and say something like, "I recognize you are not coming from me, and you are not coming from my God. I stand against you, and I am telling you to leave me immediately, according to the wisdom of God that say's when I submit to God, he gives me the power to resist the evil one." If you do this enough, those negative thoughts will no longer become a runway for the enemy to take up space in your heart. It is of the utmost importance that you fill your mind with what God says about you, because what you agree with has power over you. There are so many good things that God has to tell you, and his love will build a runway that is meant for him alone. It will be the place where God is no longer distant. You withstand the enemy by standing with God in his love for you.

KEY POINTS

1. Believe God speaks to you.
2. Trust that God is speaking to you. He will make sure you are not confused or deceived.

3. Be open to new ways he will speak.

4. Learn to live by the voice of God and not the voice of others.

5. If needed, invite the counsel of those who are more mature with God's ways and his Word to bring clarity.

ACTIVATION

Take a piece of paper and a pen and write down this question for God:

"What are your thoughts for me right now?"

Begin to still yourself and focus on the God who loves you and wants to speak to you. For any distracting thoughts, write those down on another piece of paper. Waiting on God is active; it means we activate our faith believing that God is going to speak. The first thought that comes to your mind that is loving, kind, encouraging, comforting, or hopeful write down. When you are done, go back and read it back to God. Thank him for what he has spoken to you.

There is a voice out there that is God's. He wants to live in you and empower you to live the life you are called to live. Your story isn't over, and your portrait is still being developed. The role that God has for you is designed to fit you perfectly. Once you begin to hear what that is, you will not want to live any other life. You are beautiful in every facet of your being. May you be empowered to take this journey called "Life with God" and find your ultimate purpose, passion, and destiny. You will find the life you were meant to live with God, yourself, and others. Go for it. You've got this, girl

Conclusion

Chapter 9
LIVING IN REST

REST ASSURED

Sometimes the most spiritual thing you can do is rest. Living is rest is not simply that we take naps or get eight hours of sleep. Rather, the rest I am talking about is the permission we give ourselves knowing that everything doesn't depend on us. Life with me, living with others, and living with God all require intention, energy, and the activation of a faith-filled life. Finding a place to rest our minds, emotions, and bodies will not only refuel us and refresh us but can become the space we retreat to when we find that we are running on overload.

God wants for us to have good self-care, so that we are around for the long haul. "Life with me" means we can do our best to fill our lives with skills, talents, and experiences, make really good choices, spend time with those who value us, and then trust God to see where Jesus leads us. We need "life with others" who can see our potential. Those who can see us higher than we see ourselves, who have a vision that is greater than we thought possible. We need to clean up the messes of those who have hurt us or where we have hurt others. We need a "life with God" who holds the blueprint. We need to hear his voice so he can stir us to live with purpose and passion, love and faith. Living with God means that we can rest in the fact that he has our lives in the palm of his hands.

This is the joy of a God-ordained life that is so much more than fate and luck. It is intentional, purposeful, and can be full of the one who holds destiny in his hands. We don't have to have everything figured out. We can enjoy this journey called life and place our hope, trust, and process in the hands of the one who is faithful. We can live out of who we really are and invite wisdom that comes from above and from those who have a history of walking with God. "I am confident that the Creator, who has begun such a great work among you, will *not stop in mid-design but will* keep perfecting you until the day Jesus the Anointed, *our Liberating King, returns to redeem the world.*"[1] We need God, we need others, and we need to be who we are called to be.

REMEMBER TO REST

Life can be overwhelming. "When life is over whelming, we can tell God every detail of our life and God's wonderful peace will keep your thoughts and your heart quiet and at rest as you trust in Christ Jesus.[2] Everyday life has a way of getting in the way of our spiritual life with God. Our jobs, our duties, our relationships, and our own schedules can leave us exhausted and without internal rest. We can spend so much time doing life that we forget to tap into the Source of all life. God tells us not to be anxious, and we can do that by going back into our "tent in the woods" and surrendering to him. We can offer up our prayers, giving him our grateful hearts and, if need be, offering a sacrifice of worship. It is a sacrifice to worship and trust God when we don't feel like it. We can put into practice the meaning of the tabernacle and once again find the peace and presence of God.

> Do not be anxious about anything, but in every situation, by prayer and petition, with thanksgiving, present your requests to God. And the peace of God, which transcends all understanding, will guard your hearts and your minds in Christ Jesus. Finally, brothers and sisters, whatever is true, whatever is noble, whatever is right, whatever is pure, whatever is lovely, whatever is admirable—if anything is excellent or praiseworthy—think about such things. Whatever you have learned or received or heard from me or seen in me—put it into practice. And the God of peace will be with you.[3]

Excess busyness will always lead us away from God. I have been active, hardworking, committed, and enthusiastic, which are all excellent qualities that have helped me to have a successful life. But they are not a guarantee that things will always go well for me. There are times I find myself out of sync with the world around me, and I can feel myself spinning on the inside. Going around in circles internally will eventually cause me to spiral downward until I am stressed out, burnt out, and overwhelmed. I always thought I could do anything I put my mind to. As I grew into adulthood, my active outgoing personality started to kick up a notch, as I quickly became like the "Energizer Bunny," a marketing icon from a popular commercial from Energizer batteries that showed a robotic bunny moving around beating a drum that never died out. My high-energy love of people and love of life caused me to need supercharged batteries to keep up with the demands I allowed others to place upon the ones I already put on myself.

My drive to keep going at times caused me to outrun my today in preparation for tomorrow, and I forgot to live in the moment. I put myself on the treadmill of life running faster and faster until I forgot what it meant to rest. I started to feel more like a hamster running on a wheel in a cage, than a person running toward my destiny. I would feel guilty about taking time for myself, and the word *rest* was not in my vocabulary. The closer I got to God and the more time I spent with him, the quieter I got on the inside and that started showing up on the outside. As I learned to sit and journal with God and listen to what he has to say to me, the more restful I became, and one day I heard the voice of God say to me that "Everything good flows from a place of rest." I knew in that moment I needed to learn to live from rest.

CARVING OUT TIME TO REST

Finding God helped me to find rest and to connect with the stillness of who was living on the inside of me. My relationship with God helped me to find true peace. Stillness to me isn't sitting back and doing nothing, it is living from the heart of God. It is living an intentional life that has built into it the ability to live from a place of rest. Rest is not simply a break from the busyness of life; it is found in the one who is on the inside of me and in knowing God and knowing who I am. The world will pressure you to conform to its standard of excellence. God will walk with you exactly where you are and take you into greater identity and purpose. He will take you off the treadmill of life and put you on the path to destiny.

Jesus taught us, "And everything I've taught you is so that the peace which is in me will be in you and will give you great confidence as you rest in me. For in this unbelieving world, you will experience trouble and sorrows, but you must be courageous, for I have conquered the world!"[4] Having Jesus in my life has made me aware of the peace and life that dwells inside of me. He has taught me to live from a place of rest. There are some keys I have learned that have helped me find rest from within.

Through Meditation

Meditation is a common tool for stress. Meditation has become the answer to the anxiety and stress that has plagued a generation. What really is meditation? Meditation has been defined by the culture as finding a place to focus and center ourselves on our surroundings—trusting in the floor that supports us, learning to let go, relax and turn back to the breath. With each exhalation, we are to become a little more relaxed and softer. And each inhalation is supposed to bring in peace, happiness, and quiet. The goal is to take in peace, and if the mind wanders, which it will, we are instructed to bring it back to our breath. This usually requires some kind of mediator leading the guided meditation, such as soft music, a podcast on meditation, or a spiritual teacher who leads you into your inner self. This has helped many people unhook from the world and find rest.

This kind of tool is very helpful to slow down our breathing. Meditation has a far deeper meaning for me. It has to do with my focus. I have found that when my focus is on me, I begin to analyze myself. I judge whether I am breathing deep enough, or if my mind is really able to quiet down. Focusing on my breath keeps me so self-focused that I am made aware of my own poor evaluation of myself, and my breathing distracts me to where I only receive a partial measure of peace. I am usually thinking too much, and I am never able to fully let go of the things of the day. I need to have a focus other than myself.

Biblical meditation is different. It requires us to focus on the delight of God's Word, his nature, and his ways. Our focus in not only physical (such as our breath) but also spiritual as we focus on who God says he is. The psalmist in Psalm 1:1–3 speaks of those who spend time with God's Word. Not because they feel like they are supposed to, but because they take delight in hearing from God through his Word. They are like trees planted by living waters that yield their fruit in their proper season. To meditate is to think about what you are reading, to study it and share with others what you are gleaning, and allow it to take root in your heart. It is from this place of deep rootedness in God's truth that produces fruit in our lives. We can also receive the blessing of health and consistent growth that comes as we meditate on the Word of God. Sometimes I will take something I have read and will spend weeks pondering what God is speaking to me.

We can develop the practice of pondering as a spiritual discipline of meditation. I am reminded of Mary, the mother of Jesus, when the birth of God's Son was foretold to her. The first time an angel spoke to her, Mary pondered and wondered what this could mean.[5] Pondering is a way of bringing together in one's mind; to mentally consider, to converse with, to meet with, to consider.[6] Sometimes we, too, can ponder what it is that God's has said and is saying to us and allow it to take root in our hearts. To meditate on God's Word is to think about a promise, a passage, or a story. As you ponder that in your heart, you will gain greater understanding of what God is saying to you and how you can apply his truth to every situation in your life. Focusing on God's Word becomes the breath you need to flourish.

Biblical meditation includes God's Word and God's Spirit. To meditate is to sit and chew and embrace the Word of God until it becomes a part of who we are. Wisdom comes in the stillness and quietness of meditating on God's Word. This is where true wisdom is burst in you through the power of the Holy Spirit. This is the kind of wisdom that knows how to bring solutions to the problems and discrepancies around us. It is this kind of meditation that reorders our minds, our will, and our emotions and brings contentment, peace, and tranquility. Meditating on the breath can calm your body down, but many times what we are thinking causes us stress. Biblical meditation renews our minds so that we can learn to think like God and can bring the peace that transcends our own understanding. It is through biblical meditation that we can see a generation thrive in health, wholeness, and prosperity. This is God's antidote to your stress, chaos, and the problems of the world, which is much more than what the world offers in the form of meditation.

When my focus is on Jesus, my breathing slows down naturally in response to the presence of peace, because that is who his is. When I posture my heart to the fact that Jesus is there in my midst, he inspires, empowers, and gives me purpose. God's promise is this: "You will keep him in perfect peace, whose mind is stayed on You, because he trusts in You."[7] As I trust that God is with me and look for him, it's like he is standing in front of me breathing over me with the words "Be at peace, I am right here." My heart is stilled, and I find peace.

Through Creativity

We can also find rest and the presence of peace through the creative works of God. Peace is as much a mindset, as it is the action of acknowledging God through his creative nature. Many find rest in spending time outside in the beauty and landscape of the earth. Some find peace in a creative idea that brings about a much-needed solution. Creativity in the form of the arts and music, poetry, and the printed canvas are practical ways in which we put God's creative nature on display.

I have heard of stories where an artist painted a picture in which a person was given the piece of art, and it brought healing to their heart. The painting activated the peace and knowledge of God. Writing and journaling are other ways we can experience the peace of God. When I take time out to write what is on my heart, my words on paper release what is in me. Then I can ask God a question and write what he has placed in my heart. God has a way of bringing order to the chaos inside of me through journaling. Even if you don't journal or aren't a skilled artist, spending time outside, writing, or drawing can bring life to the canvas. Even if it is the canvas of your soul that needs refreshment. Poetry can bring out the emotion of the heart, and music is soothing to the soul. Meditating on the creative works of God can give us a greater understanding of what God is saying to us through the beauty of art.

Through God's Word

I can read God's Word as a form of meditation. Here is my strategy for cultivating peace. I start with a Scripture verse that relates to what I am looking to build into my life, for example, how to be still. In the verse in Psalm 46: "Be still and know that I am God," I take each word and chew on it until I gain revelation and understanding. I start with the first word or two. "Be still" becomes a time where I make an appointment with God, each day at a specific time. I take a break from my daily routine, to take myself out of the demands of the world around me and still myself before God. I look for what I need in God's Book of Life. I may dialogue with God, pray, or listen to some music. They are all ways to settle my heart and quiet my mind to focus on God.

Strategy 1:

"Be still"—Find a comfortable place where I can get quiet. I start with a few minutes of allowing my body to rest, my heart to quiet, and my mind to focus on one verse. If I don't schedule this time, someone or something else will schedule it for me.

Strategy 2:

"And know"—This is where I quiet my mind to listen to what God has to show me, either through his Word, a thought in my mind, or the experience of an emotion, such as love, peace, joy, or sorrow. The goal is to listen.

Strategy 3:

"I am God"—This is the focus of my be-still time. A connection with God is my ultimate goal. This time is not about me trying to do anything or be anything. My only responsibility during this time is to obey what God shows me, even if that is to sit in his presence and enjoy his peace for that moment. That is more than enough because he has everything I need and is not concerned about the things that have me caught up in doing.

Strategy 4:

Dialogue with God. I start a conversation with God, as if I were talking to a friend, a mentor, or a father. I can start by thanking him for the ability to spend a few quiet moments with him, when the hustle and bustle of life is screaming for my attention. Even moments of gratitude with God can help me find rest and stillness. As I grow in cultivating stillness, I become led (by God) instead of driven. My "be still" times can be times when I evaluate my life, my current situation, and look to my future. These kinds of questions don't usually get answered in the busyness of life.

Here are three of my favorite questions to dialogue with God:

- Who do you say I am?
- Where am I now in my life?

- Where do you want me to be: in six months, a year, five years?

Through Spiritual Encounters

Sometimes when you still yourself before God and allow him to breathe life into you, you can get a picture in your mind's eye. My first encounter with a vision came as a message of truth from God. I got this picture that I had not been thinking about. I knew it was from God because it came to show me something about myself that I had not known before. It came suddenly, as if God were right there with me. It was the picture of two opened-faced hands that I knew were mine. They were held out in front of my body with my palms facing upward being offered up to God. All ten fingers were spread apart—I saw my opened palms facing up to the heavens—then the picture became alive as I saw what looked like sand running down through all of my fingers and falling to the ground. I instantly knew this was God showing me something, and it came with the interpretation.

The Holy Spirit is the one who leads us into all truth. This vision came with the truth of God wrapped around it, and the truth was I had held tightly all the ways I had built my life around what I was doing. I was in charge of my life, and I held everything in the palms of my own hands. Most of what I was holding on to were things I did for God. I felt the need to keep helping others and serving where I could. I was doing my best to be what I thought was a good woman and doing what God wanted. When this vision came it was as if God was asking me to let go of all that I held so tightly in my hands and lay them down for the *life that he had for me*!

Would I lay down my ministry, my leadership position, the things through which I found my value and identity? It felt like I was giving up my whole identity. My heart sank because I longed to be obedient, and yet my mind started counting the cost. I would lose the status of being a leader, and I would disappoint the other leaders who had worked so hard at developing relationship with me. I would lose the close-knit community that we had built. I would have to admit to everyone that I was not only stepping down but leaving what I had spent years building. I would be giving up my gifts and talents to do what? At the time, I thought it meant to be alone. I wish I could tell you that I immediately obeyed God. The truth is that it took over nine months to follow through and do what I knew God was asking me to do. I believe today that those nine months were the time needed to birth in me the courage to trust God and to get the wise counsel of those more mature than I was at the time. The truth is that I only knew how to "do" for God. I had no idea that I was being invited into my destiny, which started with trusting God.

Visions help us to experience God. It's one thing to know about God, and it is another thing to actually know him by experience. There is nothing more life giving than letting go of the things we "do" to connect to God and to rest long enough to experience the palpable, noticeable, tangible presence of God. It is simply undeniable. I finally walked away from the things I was doing for God for a time.

During this season of detaching myself from the life I had once built, I became more attached to God than ever before, as I learned the power of stillness and rest. I learned how to hear his voice. I learned how to process my emotions with God in a real authentic way, and the most significant thing about this experience is that I now know when I have fallen out of the peace that God provides for me. I have learned to recognize when I am being driven by what I do and not being led by God. I now use peace as my gauge in which I can recognize if I am being driven or if I am being led. It has been what's saved me in the most difficult times of my life. I have learned many ways to meditate on God, which has brought me so much peace.

LEARNING TO QUIET THE MIND

The hardest part I think about finding rest is being still with ourselves. Our minds race, and we think about all the things of the day, which really consist of just the basics of life. I know for many, the hardest part will be all of the commitments, deadlines, and responsibilities we have. Who has the time to just hang out and spend time with God? The truth is that if we are too busy for God, we will not get what we need to deal with all of the busyness of life. Sometimes we just have to take ourselves off the treadmill of life and spend some time alone with God.

Setting aside even ten minutes a day will refocus you. If you are having a hard time quieting your mind, you can make a list of all the things that are running through your mind, and by writing them down, you have given them a place of rest. You can put them aside, knowing you can address those things later. The list will be there when you are done, and the likelihood is much greater that they will actually get done because you have been revived.

Stillness will bring you into his presence that offers peace, which brings order and alignment to your emotions, thinking, and choices, so that you become whole in spirit, soul, and body.[8] It is in cultivating stillness that you can learn to dial down your emotions, settle your mind, and rest your body. You may also find that God shows you his truth. "This is how we know that we belong to the truth and how we set our hearts at rest in His presence"[9] Everything that flows out of rest can become the very thing that God uses to bring you closer to your destiny. Rest changes everything.

MAKING IT REAL

I invite you to hear the Lord's invitation to be still and know that he is God. You can pray the following prayer and simply "rest" in his presence. Imagine yourself sitting by the quiet movement of the sound of a slow-running stream. The sun is out, and there is not a soul around. It is just you and God. You are sitting on the lush grass and can feel the refreshment of a cool light breeze brushing across your still body bringing you complete comfort. Speak to yourself, "Be still my soul and trust in the Lord."

ACTIVATION

Recite and meditate on Psalm 131:1–2:

> Lord, my heart is meek before you,
>
> I don't consider myself better than others.
>
> I'm content to not pursue matters that are over my head
>
> Such as your complex mysteries and wonders that I'm not yet ready to understand.
>
> I am humbled and quieted in your presence,
>
> Like a contented child who rests on its mother's lap,
>
> I'm your resting child and my soul is content in you.[10]

Chapter 10
EMBRACING LIFE

WRAPPING IT UP

There are some things you may need to pack up and close up as you step into the beauty of who you were meant to be. As you step into your God-given reality, you will find there is something distinctive and special on God's heart for you to become. There are some things that are distracting you from becoming all that you were meant to be. Saying "good-bye" to those people, places, or things doesn't have to be dramatic. It will take knowing what season you are in. It will take courage to step out of one season and into another; it will require a new destination. Once you begin to see yourself as God sees you—with beauty, value, and purpose—it becomes easier to recognize what you will need to let go of and what you will need to embrace.

KNOW YOUR SEASON

Every aspect of life has its season. Knowing your season allows you to know what to say yes to and what to say no to. Seasons cycle through our lives in a divine order, allowing us the time and space to grow. You can't manipulate the times and seasons, as they are God's domain. "To everything there is a season, and a time for every purpose under the Heaven."[1] Some seasons are short, and some seasons are long. Knowing which season God has you in will provide the clarity needed to live exactly where you need to be. Living in the moment can cause fear and anxiety when you are in a difficult season of growth, because without perspective it can seem like there is no way out. But if we can partner with God in the season we are in, we can navigate through the cold dark days of winter knowing that spring will come. Whether you are in the wrong season or shifting into a new season, it is important to understand which season you are fully in. How do you know your season? Let's look at what the four seasons of life can look like metaphorically:

Spring

- A time for sowing seeds, whether in relationships, jobs, financially, or in faith
- A time for new things to spring up, new strategies, new opportunities, or new relationships
- A time for planting and aiming for the stars and reaching goals

Summer

- A time for yielding fruit. Seeing the good in relationships, jobs, or life in general

- A time to enjoy the long, slower days whether in taking much-needed time away or spending much-needed time with others
- A time to enjoy the beautiful sunsets and be awakened to the rising of the sun
- A time for valuing what you accomplished and looking forward to what you are producing

Fall

- A time to gather resources, people, or skills that are needed for a long winter
- A time to see the beauty of change all around you
- A time to let what needs to die fall to the ground
- A time of deconstruction and interruption

Winter

- A time to settle into the warmth of being at home with yourself
- A time to gain greater understanding, gain new insights, and learn new skills
- A time to ride out the storms

Knowing your season is important because each season prepares you for the next season. If you are living in the wrong season, you will not see the fruit that comes from being in the right season in the right time. It is impossible to be in all the seasons at one time, as we cannot do all things at the same time. For example, you can't embrace something new, until you are willing to let go of the old you are holding on to.

Everything has its own time. If we can understand that every season of our lives has its proper time, we can see that what is needed in the current season is given in the previous season. If you can plant seeds of friendship in spring, you can enjoy the companionship of relaxing summer days at the beach. When possessing our promised future, we don't want to be left wishing we were somewhere else. It is the difficulty that is literally built into the process of riding out a storm that builds strength and character and shows us who is with us to get us to the other side. We can't wish we could go back to where we were. Otherwise, we will never get to the intended future that God has for us.

Remember that the difficulties of life prove what has been placed inside of us and what we are made of. God has made you resilient, not because you have to be strong, but because he is with you. If we don't recognize the life season we are in as well as the provision that is provided now, we will fail to step into the next season.

I love how practical God's Word is and how we can apply it to our lives. I have listed side by side the contrasting effect of how God illustrates and balances the cycles. These seasons can be used to create meaning and elicit a response from us to keep us in the right frame of mind with the right intent at the right time. The seasons are intentionally placed side by side to show us the differences. I use this as a template to describe the season I am currently in. Sometimes we can get tripped up on words like *kill*.

For example, a time to kill can be a little concerning for us, but it is a reality and appropriate during a time of war. When defending our country against terrorism, killing evil is considered an act of war. Metaphorically for us, there may be some beliefs and behaviors that are killing us and some of our relationships. It may look like you are in a season to kill or destroy those lies that have held you back, so that you can enter the season to heal your heart through forgiveness. Don't allow your own interpretation of the words that are used to describe a season to distract you; rather, ask God to speak to you what that means for you right now. Learning your season will prepare you for the next season. What season are you in?

Ecclesiastes 3:1–8

There is a time for everything,
and a season for every activity under the heavens:
a time to be born and a time to die,
a time to plant and a time to uproot,
a time to kill and a time to heal,
a time to tear down and a time to build,
a time to weep and a time to laugh,
a time to mourn and a time to dance,
a time to scatter stones and a time to gather them,
a time to embrace and a time to refrain from embracing,
a time to search and a time to give up,
a time to keep and a time to throw away,
a time to tear and a time to mend,
a time to be silent and a time to speak,
a time to love and a time to hate,
a time for war and a time for peace.[2]

There is a lot to consider here, as God has given us a desire to know the present and hope for the future. He does everything just right and on time, but we cannot completely understand what he is doing. We can, however, enjoy where we are because we trust in God. God wants us to be happy and enjoy the life that he has given us to live, because this is his gift to you and me.

STEPPING INTO THE LIFE
YOU WERE MEANT TO LIVE

Living from how God sees you frees you up to step into a new identity and become the person you were always meant to be. When your identity is in Christ, you are becoming more and more like God each day. You are more loving, kind, and considerate of others more than you consider yourself. You are less selfish and more God centered and others centered. God wants to use you to be a light, a voice of clarity, a beacon of hope, and a picture of beauty to those he brings across your path.

He will trust you to do it because you have learned to love, value, and honor who God is, who God has created you to be, and what is possible for others. It is this kind of light that shines brightly, so that others can see that there is a place in the love of God, where you can love yourself and learn how to love others. God wants you to be identified by how he sees you, so that you can grow into a light that shines and makes the world a better place

DREAM BIG

Every God-given dream can be traced back to one purpose, connection. Connection to God and connection with the world around us. Section One was all about "Life with Myself." It was about meeting our own desires for significance through our unique gift sets, personalities, and even the meaning of our names. Section Two was about our need to address the things that makes living with others messy. We learned how to clean up our messes through the power of forgiveness and the importance of surrounding ourselves with those who see us better than we see ourselves. In Section Three, we were encouraged to step beyond living for just ourselves and how we can find our significance in Christ and carry his light to the world around us. I believe that God has placed inside each of us the desire to dream beyond our own desires and passions to a life that is significant beyond our current situation and relationships to the place that God has dreamed for us.

There is a place in your spirit that is designed to connect with God and connect with others in a creative way. There is a place deep inside of you that was "created" to be an expression of heaven to the world and people around you. The very first thing that was written down for us about God is the history of creation: "In the beginning God created everything: the heavens above and the earth below."[3] Out of nothingness with the sound of his voice, creation takes form, chaos yields to order, light eclipses darkness, and emptiness fills with life.[4] This reveals to us that God is Creator and that is not all. "Then God said, 'Let Us make human beings in our image, make them, reflecting our nature, so they can be responsible for…the earth itself'…and God blessed them: 'Prosper! Reproduce! Fill the earth! Take charge!'"[5]

God, our Creator, made us to be creative and blessed us to be the trustees of his estate called Earth. We are not only to care for the earth and its inhabitants but fill the earth. He told us to take charge of how we are going to live. I believe the way we can take charge is to become who God says we are and fill the earth with his glory and splendor that is displayed through you and me. God has created us with creativity in our DNA, and when we allow his design to become who we are, we, too, can be creative. The problem is that sometimes we want to leave creativity to the artist, the designers, the inventors, and musicians. There is an artist inside of each of you that longs to express the beauty of heaven.

For many, that place of creativity can be locked up inside of them, and it is longing to come out. Your gifts, talents, imagination, personality, and expression are all forms of creativity. I can envision some of you creating heaven on earth by using your gift of hospitality by inviting others over, pulling out your culinary skills, and providing an inviting place for others to feel at home in your presence. Heaven can look like being at home with each other and at home in God's creation. I see others taking their organization skills and providing a place of peace and calm for those around them. Heaven can look like peace and order.

I see others of you taking the gifts and talents that you have discovered and not simply making a career out of them but building and creating a place of value for others. Heaven can look like honor, respect, and kindness. Every human heart and every human spirit have an element of the expression that God has chosen to use to display creativity. If you have disqualified yourself, I call you back to dream again. Take your gifts, your talents, and your personality, and imagine how you could make the world a better place. Then allow yourself to dream again. You can take your unique creativity and invite those around you into the beauty of God. You are created to be a display of God's splendor and beauty.

God's ultimate purpose for our lives is to join him in the ongoing work of creation. Through relationship, we can reflect God's relational richness and come back to a place of expressing the beauty and creativity of heaven on earth. God wants to use you to express his beauty to the world around you. He wants you to dream again. Not just for yourself this time, rather to show the world what a life with God can really look like. God has a plan and a future for all of humanity that is for good, but it is not automatic. Everyone can dream, but many people can't visualize it, act on it, and achieve it.

We discovered in section "Life with Myself" some of the areas on which God has put his grace. You may not have grown up believing in God, or maybe you don't have believers in your family, but there can be family gifts, talents, and traits that are waiting for you to believe God for and pick them up and take them back so you can ask God to put his grace on them to become a gift to the world. Your possibilities with God are endless. As hard as it is for us to wrap our minds around the idea that life is more than fate or karma, it is true that God knows you, and he has put you on earth at this moment in time to accomplish what he knew the world would need. You are his dream come true.

MAKING IT REAL

God wants to take your dream and help you define it. Making a dream chart is a creative way to define what is in your heart. One of the best ways to dream with God is to write down those things that are in your heart and begin to own them as part of your life story. The prophet Habakkuk had learned the importance of writing down clearly the vision that the Lord had showed him so that whoever read it could run with it. His words are clear it is not yet time for the vision to come true, but that time is coming soon. It may seem like a long time, but be patient and wait for it, because it will surely come. It will not be delayed.[6]

The words of the prophet Habakkuk inspired me to write down my own vision for my life. I was encouraged to wait for the dream, and if it was from God, it would be bigger than me, and it would be for others to run with after me. God promises that it may take a long time, but it will surely come. Many people can wait and expect their dreams to come true. One of the ways I chose to act on my dream was to create my own dream board. I took old pictures from magazines, flyers that came in the mail, and images off of the computer that represented who I was, what I cared about, and what I wanted to see happen in my life. I included things like the house I always wanted, things that I love to do, and I also included a picture of young women sitting around in a circle, which I placed next to a picture of myself.

I always dreamed of having young women around me where I could take what I had learned, fought for, and received by grace and give it to them for free. This drawing became a vision for my life that I could step into. I love the TEDtalk by Patti Dobrowolski called "Drawing your Future."[7] I encourage you to watch this episode where Patti shows how when we draw our future and take three bold steps—see it, believe it, and act on it—we can see our future happen. She includes inviting others into our lives to support us in our visions. You don't need to only be inspired by a dream; you can become the person of your dream.

You may not fulfill every aspect of your dream immediately, but living in the reality of your dream takes a step of activation. Let me explain what I mean. I was with a friend the other day, and I asked her what her dream was for the next five years. She began to share what was on her heart. One thing was to move to the West Coast; we were living on the East Coast. I challenged her to begin to activate her dream by looking at real estate in the town she dreamed of living in. I shared my own dream board that I had made and how it took three years, some wise counsel, a life coach, and hearing from God for me to sell my home and move across the country to be near my children.

My dream wasn't automatic, but as I began to write out what the Lord was showing me, I was able to look at my life for areas that I was able to see where I consistently live out part of my dream. I was able to see how many times young women come to me for mentoring, spiritual guidance, and hope for a bright future. I took a risk to step out and do something to partner with my dream, waited, and it came true. This book is part of my dream. The key in waiting is to be active or to wait expectantly by inviting the resources and wise counsel of others into our dreams. I encouraged my friend with this story and challenged her to write out or draw a picture of what had been placed in her heart; otherwise, I could sit with her in this same spot five years from now and find her still in the same place of her life waiting for her dream to begin. It is important to write it so we can see it, believe it, and act on it.

START LIVING NOW

A successful life always starts on the inside. What we do doesn't make us who we are. When we know who we are and who we belong to, we have the beginnings of a life on purpose. It starts with getting what's on the inside right. When we can get our internal lives in a place of divine order, we will find the strength we need to make it through any season. We will also have the courage to step out and become who God has said we are. Even if the world around us is in chaos and full of fear, we can trust that God is with us, and together we can make it through the storms. God is always taking us to a place of greater purpose, strength, and wholeness. God gives us his supernatural ability within us that continually pushes us forward into our future and past our greatest fears. And even if we fall, God will brush us off and encourage us to get back up and keep going because we have a dream to fulfill.

God right now, by his Holy Spirit, is shedding light on his love for you. It is not something you can orchestrate yourself; it comes by his Spirit. This Spirit is definable, explainable, powerful, and tangible. This is the God who is Spirit and who is seen through the model of Jesus, who has given us the way, the truth, and the language to experience life in a whole new way. God loves you, and it is our greatest privilege to know and experience life to the fullest, which is to be filled with the fullness of God. It is out of this place of being filled with the essence of God that you can become a dream come true. One last time, stop where you are and take a moment and breathe in the breath of God, and hear him say to your heart: "I am your God." It is living in the light of this reality that you can catch the true heart of God and follow him by faith into your destiny. God is here. Turn on the light.

ABOUT THE AUTHOR

Cathy Tonking is an author and activator whose greatest desire is to help a generation know and experience God as he really is. For many years, she worked in her local church where she built and ran a café where people could connect to God and each other in a practical way.

Since 2002, she has ministered in the area of healing of the whole person, whether it is emotional healing, physical healing, or renewing the mind with the Word of God. She is a mentor, trainer, and is known best as "Mama Cathy."

Cathy loves her husband, their adult children, and grandchildren. They reside in Arizona and enjoy traveling, boating, and spending time with family and friends.

ENDNOTES

INTRODUCTION

1. Proverbs 4:23, NIV
2. Isaiah 46:3-4, TPT
3. Proverbs 4:18, TPT
4. Proverbs 13:22, ESV

CHAPTER 1

1. Ephesians 3:15, NIV
2. Hicks, Bethany. "Own Your Assignment", Independently published, 2019.
3. Breland, Jeremy. "Abram to Abraham? Why did He do it?" *Walterboro Live*, June 28, 2020. www.walterborolive.com/stories/abram-to-abraham-why-did-he-do-it-faith,32425.
4. Genesis 17:5, TLB
5. Genesis 32:28, MSG

CHAPTER 2

1. James 1:17, NKJV
2. Smalley, Gary & Norma, and Trent, John & Cindy, "*The Treasure Tree,*" Thomas Nelson Books, 1992.

3. Dr. John Trent's Strong Family Website, www.strongfamilies. com/store *The Treasure Tree* - product description.

4. Smalley, Gary & Norma, Trent, John & Cindy. "*The Treasure Tree*," Thomas Nelson Books, 1992, p. 107.

CHAPTER 3

1. Ephesians 2:10b, TPT
2. Romans 8:28, NIV
3. Genesis 1:31, NIV
4. Genesis 12:1-3, NIV
5. Jeremiah 29:11, NIV
6. Jeremiah 29:13, NIV
7. Ephesians 2:10, TPT
8. Philippians 1:4–6, TPT

CHAPTER 4

1. 1 John 3:4, MSG
2. Romans 3:23–24, The Amplified Bible, Classic Edition
3. Luke 23:34, NKJV
4. Matthew 6:15, NIV
5. Cited in Cook, E. T. *The Life of Florence Nightingale.* (1913). Vol 1, p. 237.
6. Luke 23:34, NIV
7. Ephesians 4:32, NIV
8. John 16:33, TPT

CHAPTER 5

1. TOZER, A.W. "*The Knowledge of the Holy*", August 12, 2012, Fig-Books, p. 4.
2. John 1:12, TPT

3. Romans 8:31, NKJV
4. Ephesians, 2:10, TPT
5. Hebrews 4:15, TPT
6. John 10:30, NIV
7. "G1520 – heis – Strong's Greek Lexicon (NIV)." Bible Hub. Monday, 15 February 2021.
8. Psalm 139:23–24, TPT

CHAPTER 6

1. Luke 2:8–11, NIV
2. Revelation 5:11–12, paraphrased
3. Daniel 3:28, paraphrased
4. Luke 1:30, paraphrased
5. Psalm 91:11, NKJV
6. Psalm 34:7, NKJV
7. 1 John 1:5, NKJV
8. 1 John 2:11, NKJV
9. Luke 2:14, NKJV
10. Isaiah 45:19, MSG
11. Philippians 4:8, MSG
12. Exodus 3:14, NIV
13. www.thomasnelsonbibles.com/jesus-seven-i-am-statements/
14. 1 Samuel 30:8, New American Standard Bible
15. Jeremiah 29:13–14, NIV

CHAPTER 7

1. Matthew 18:20, NIV
2. Exodus 33:11, NIV
3. Romans 12:1–2, NCV
4. Philippians 4:8, MSG

5. Exodus 38:8, NIV
6. Hebrews 1:3, TPT
7. Matthew 11:29, NIV, paraphrased
8. John 6:35, NIV
9. Matthew 14:13–21, NIV
10. Psalm 34:8, NKJV
11. John 8:12, NIV
12. Matthew 5:16, TPT
13. Psalm 141:2, NIV
14. Matthew 27:50–51, TPT
15. Ezekiel 36:26, NIV
16. Ephesians 2:21, TPT

CHAPTER 8

1. John 10:27, NLJV
2. Proverbs 3:5–6, NKJV
3. Romans 12:2 NCV
4. 1 Corinthians 2:9, NIV
5. Jeremiah 33:3, NIV
6. Proverbs 2:6, ESV
7. 1 Samuel 3:9, NIV
8. 1 Kings, 19:11-13, NKJV
9. Virkler, Dr. Mark Introduces 4 Keys to Hearing God's Voice, www.cwgministries.org/Four-Keys-to-Hearing-Gods-Voice
10. Matthew 6:21–22, TPT
11. Proverbs 3:5-6, NKJV
12. Isaiah 9:6, NIV
13. Romans 10:10 NCV
14. James 4:7, TPT

CHAPTER 9

1. Philippians 1:6, The Voice
2. Philippians 4:7, TLB
3. Philippians 4:6-8, NIV
4. John 16:33, TPT
5. Luke 2:19, NKJV
6. "G4820 - symballō - Strong's Greek Lexicon (kjv)." Blue Letter Bible. Web. 25 Jun, 2021. www.blueletterbible.org/lexicon/g4820/kjv/tr/0-1.
7. Isaiah 26:3, NKJV
8. 3 John 1:2, paraphrased
9. 1 John 3:19, NIV
10. Psalm 131:1–2, TPT

CHAPTER 10

1. Ecclesiastes 3:1, NKJV
2. Ecclesiastes 3:1–8, NIV
3. Genesis 1:1, NIV
4. Genesis 1:1, The Voice, notes preceding the verse
5. Genesis 1:26–28, MSG
6. Habakkuk 2:2–3, NCV
7. www.youtube.com/watch?v=A7KRSCyLqc4

Made in United States
North Haven, CT
20 October 2021